Fellowship Farm 1

Books 1-3

Melanie Lotfali

THE FITZGERALDS

FLEA, FLEX & FIZZ

VISITORS ARRIVE

BOOK ONE

THE FITZGERALDS

Leezah, Skye-Maree and Olingah Fitzgerald live with their parents on Fellowship Farm. In this, the first book of the Fellowship Farm series, we meet the children and learn about their daily activities on the farm.

There is a lot to be done each day: pillow fights, morning prayers, pig feeding and school bus riding...

Join them as they help their dad feed the cows, add stickers to their virtues poster and learn to deal with bullies. Then follow the adventures of your new friends from Fellowship Farm in the other books of the series.

PRAISE AND GRATITUDE

All praise, O my God, be to Thee Who art the Source of all glory and majesty, of greatness and honor, of sovereignty and dominion, of loftiness and grace, of awe and power. Whomsoever Thou willest Thou causest to draw nigh unto the Most Great Ocean, and on whomsoever Thou desirest Thou conferrest the honor of recognizing Thy Most Ancient Name. Of all who are in heaven and on earth, none can withstand the operation of Thy sovereign Will. From all eternity Thou didst rule the entire creation, and Thou wilt continue for evermore to exercise Thy dominion over all created things. There is none other God but Thee, the Almighty, the Most Exalted, the All-Powerful, the All-Wise.

Illumine, O Lord, the faces of Thy servants, that they may behold Thee; and cleanse their hearts that they may turn unto the court of Thy heavenly favors, and recognize Him Who is the Manifestation of Thy Self and the Dayspring of

120

Breakfast

Leezah rolled over on her top bunk bed and looked at the clock. The clock said ten minutes to six. It was still dark but it was nearly time to get up. Leezah loved the early morning even though it was cold. She lay in her warm bed for a few more minutes. She was covered by her big warm bedspread that had waves and fish sewn on it. Her aunty and uncle had made it for her tenth birthday. At six o'clock she pushed the bedspread down to her feet and put her warm brown foot on the top wrung of the cold bunk ladder.

She slowly edged her way down the ladder trying not to make it creak too much. As she got near the bottom she felt something tickling her foot. "Hey!" she giggled and poked her foot through the ladder at her little sister. "Good morning sister," said Skye-Maree, grabbing the foot. Leezah pulled her foot free and swung herself onto her sister's bed. She pulled back the covers and started to tickle her. She giggled and struggled but her eight-year-old muscles were no match for her big sister. Luckily for Skye her giggles woke their younger brother, Olingah.

Olingah was onto Leezah's back in a flash. Soon the cold wooden boards of the bedroom floor were covered in bedspreads, and squealing, giggling, tickling children. When their mother opened the door and turned on the light, all she saw was a sea of body parts in different colored pajamas. A red elbow, a green leg, a yellow bottom. All twisted up in pillows and quilts and making very strange noises. "What have you wild animals done with my lovely children?" she asked, and left the room.

A few minutes later the panting wild-haired children picked themselves up off the floor. They put on their dressing-gowns and slippers and joined their mother and father in the living room. Their mother had turned on the lamps and lit the fire. Their father was taking the guitar out of its case. They kissed their mummy and daddy good morning and sat on the rug by the fire.

"Did you have a lovely sleep?" Daddy asked.

"Yes," said Olingah, "but now I'm hungry."

"Good, "said Mummy. "We'll have breakfast soon. But first we need to feed our...?"

"Souls!" said all the children at once.

"What would your soul like to eat?" asked Mummy

"Delicious prayers please," said Skye-Maree.

Daddy strummed the guitar and they started to sing their prayers.

When they had finished they sat quietly for a few moments, thinking about 'Abdu'l-Bahá. The fire felt warm on their backs and outside the birds were singing beautiful prayers of their own.

"My soul's full," said Olingah, "but my tummy's empty!" He scrambled up and went quickly off to the kitchen.

In the kitchen they worked as a team. Daddy cut up the fruit. Leezah and Skye toasted the toast and put out the boxes of cereal. Mummy warmed some milk and poured some juice for everyone. Olingah put out the bowls, plates, cups, spoons and knives. As they ate their breakfast the sun rose over the hills, shining down on fields of their farm.

Morning chores

The sun was bright but the air was still cold. So when they finished eating and went outside to do their chores, all five of them put on their warm coats, hats, and boots. When the children were in a rush, they divided their jobs among themselves. But when they had plenty of time they liked to do their morning work all together.

The first job was to get the scrap bucket from under the kitchen sink and take it to the pigpen. The pigpen was right down at the end of the paddock. As they walked over the grass they looked back to see the trails they had made in the dew. Skye threw the scraps into the pig trough. Leezah filled their water trough with clean water. Olingah put clean straw in their pen. It was a little bit scary for him. Olingah was only six and the two sows – mummy pigs- were bigger than him. He tried to be courageous but sometimes he needed Leezah to help him do the straw.

The next job was to feed the farm dogs. The farm dogs were tied to kennels near the big shed that housed the tractors and trucks. The children loved dogs, but they didn't like the job of feeding the farm dogs. The meaty bones that they got from the big old fridge in the shed made their hands stink. The dogs were always really hungry and pulled at their chains barking and straining to get to their food. The children threw the bones toward the dogs and while they ate, Skye washed out and filled the water dishes.

The next job was to let the hens out, feed them and collect the eggs. During the day the hens were free to wander round the farm. But at night they had to be locked in their house so that the foxes wouldn't eat them. Their house was bright yellow with three big red hens painted on the side, all laying big blue eggs. The children had helped their daddy paint it.

As Leezah went in to get the eggs, she said: "Guess how many there are. I guess there are ten eggs."

Skye-Maree said: "I guess there will be eight eggs today."

"Me too," said Olingah.

"You can't guess the same Olly," said Skye. "We all have to guess differently, that's the game."

"Oh," said Olingah. "Well I'll guess nine."

"There are eight eggs," said Leezah coming out of the henhouse with the eggs in an ice-cream container.

"Yay! I was right," said Olingah.

The children walked back towards the farmhouse. The sun was rising high above the hills now. There was just one last job left to do – feed the pigeons. Their daddy had thirty pigeons in a big cage which was really like a house. He had trained them to fly out across the farm and return to their house. The children gave the pigeons some seed. The pigeons were so tame that they would eat right out of the children's hands. It tickled when the pigeons pecked at the seed in their hands and sometimes it hurt a little bit. The rest of the seed they poured into the pigeons' dishes.

Then they raced each other across the back lawn, up the verandah steps and into the house. Leezah and Skye shook off their rubber boots, and hung up their coats and hats and gloves. Olingah's boots were getting too small for him. He shook and shook but they didn't come off. "Oh you silly boot," he cried at his boot, stuck on his foot. "Can you please help me Leezah?" he asked.

"Of course," said Leezah. "You hold Olingah, Skye, and I'll pull the boot." Together they got the stubborn boot off Olingah's foot.

"Thank you," said Olingah.

Just as they got the boot off, Daddy came up the verandah steps. "That was great helpfulness," he said to Leezah and Skye.

"And Olingah was courteous," said Skye.

"That's right! So you can all add a sticker to your virtues chart."

Leezah, Skye and Olingah went into the kitchen and got the stickers out of the second drawer. Leezah chose a sticker of a smiling green frog. Skye chose a sticker of a space ship and Olingah chose a sticker that had a big red face saying: 'Good Work'.

On the fridge was a big piece of card with the virtues written on it. Olingah stuck his sticker next the word "Courtesy" and the girls stuck theirs next to "Helpfulness". Their virtues poster was nearly full of stickers!!

The school bus

The children quickly made their beds and had their showers. When they were clean and dry they put on their school uniforms. Olingah especially loved wearing his uniform because he had only started school that year. They put on their yellow skivvies and their navy blue jumper. Then their blue pants and their white socks. Their blue leather shoes were waiting for them by the back door.

Mummy and Daddy helped them do their hair. Leezah wore her long thick black hair in plaits at night so that she wouldn't have knots in the morning. Skye's hair was so frizzy that it was always hard to get a comb through it or keep it neat. But Skye loved her frizz. Olingah's light brown hair reached down to his shoulders and was very fine and always full of knots.

The children packed their bags for school: lunch boxes, drink bottles, books and pens. Skye also took her football and Olingah took his kite. Then they gave their mummy and daddy a big hug and kiss, put on their blue duffel coats and went out to the main road to wait for the school bus. Before the bus arrived they heard the roar of the tractor and saw Mummy driving off to the back paddocks to plough. Daddy drove the white Ute over to the petrol pump. He filled the tank while he waited for the bus to arrive to collect the children.

Leezah climbed up on the front fence. She stuck her arms out to the side and balanced her way along the fence, stopping at each fat wooden fence post to regain her balance. Skye climbed up on the gate, then leapt to the ground. The whole fence shook as she pushed off into the air. Leezah wobbled and wobbled and tumbled off the fence into the long grass beside it.

"SKYE-MAREE!" she yelled

"Sorry sister!!" said Skye.

"Come on!" said Olingah. "Here comes the bus."

Actually no-one could see the bus yet but far along the road they saw a swirl of dust. As it got closer and closer they could see the old red bus in the middle of it. The children stood well back from the road as the bus pulled up and the dust cloud swirled around it. Then they climbed on board.

"Good morning Ms Rowbottom," they greeted the bus driver. Ms Rowbottom had been driving the school bus since before Leezah started at Kellyton Primary School. She was a bit grumpy sometimes. Some of the children called her Ms Paddlebum behind her back. At first Leezah and Skye thought it was really funny. But Daddy said it wasn't kind, so they stopped calling her Ms Paddlebum, even when the other children called her that name.

Because their farm was the furthest along the road, the Fitzgerald children – Leezah, Skye-Maree and Olingah – were always the first to get on the bus. As the bus journeyed back towards the township it collected children from other farms and houses along the way. The children loved the ride into school. Each time the bus stopped more friends got on. So by the time the bus reached the school it was full of noisy, playing, laughing shouting school children. No wonder Ms Rowbottom was sometimes grumpy. When the children got TOO noisy Ms Rowbottom would slam on the brakes and stop the bus.

"Right!" she would say, "Who wants to walk to school?" and open the bus door.

After that the children would try very hard to be quiet as mice. Some of them had to hold their mouths so their giggles wouldn't escape. Then Ms Rowbottom would start the bus again and continue towards the school. Within about two minutes the noise would be as bad as it was before. Somehow there was just too much to be said, too much fun to be had, to be quiet as mice!!

The bus arrived at the school at 8:10 every morning. Leezah went to her classroom with the other fifth graders. Skye went to the grade three classroom and Olingah went off with his friends from grade one.

Home time

At the end of the school day Leezah, Skye-Maree and Olingah met under the big oak trees out the front of their school. They waited with the other children to get on the school bus. The bus was always there before them but they had to wait for Ms Rowbottom to open the doors. She never let the children on until everyone was there and it was time to leave.

The Fitzgerald children were earlier than most of the others. Leezah had some money left from her pocket money. "Let's go to the shop," she called to her brother and sister.

"How much do you have Leezah?" asked Olingah.

"Fifty cents."

The children left the school grounds and went to the pedestrian crossing. The Lollipop Lady was standing at the side of the road with her big red STOP sign. When she saw the children, she checked for cars. Then, she walked out into the middle of the road and stood there with her sign. The children smiled and thanked Ms Gabriel. They walked across the road, stepping only on the fat white lines. Mummy called Ms Gabriel the Angel Gabriel because Ms Gabriel helped keep the children safe.

Inside the shop the children went to the glass counter that had boxes of different kinds of lollies behind it. Olingah was a little too short to see the lollies so he jumped up and down looking in. "What do you want?" asked Leezah.

"I'll have a red frog please," said Olingah jumping up and down where the red frog box was sitting on the shelf behind the glass.

"And I'll have five smarties," said Skye, "One of each color please."

Leezah chose two musk sticks and paid for the lollies. Then they went back to catch the bus home.

The bus drove through the little seaside town past the bank, the newsagent, and the bakery. Just before it headed out onto the road to the farms, the bus drove past the vet. Each afternoon the Fitzgeralds' orange Ute was parked out the front. Leezah, Skye and Olingah's mother was the town vet. Dr

Fitzgerald worked at the surgery every afternoon from 12:30 to 5:00pm. If she was between patients Dr Fitzgerald would come out of her surgery at 3:15 to wave to her children as they went past on the bus.

As the bus went past the surgery she appeared on the verandah. Olingah stood on his seat and stuck his head out of the window. He yelled: "Hi Mummy!! Hi Mummy!! Dr Fitzgerald grinned and waved. Ms Rowbottom yelled: "GET YOUR HEAD IN THE WINDOW OR YOU CAN WALK HOME." Skye grabbed Olingah's other arm and pulled him down onto his seat.

Some of the big kids at the back of the bus started laughing. "Hi Mummy! Hi Mummy!" they called, making silly faces and waving their arms. "Hi DAH-LEENG!!" said another, pretending to be Dr Fitzgerald. The children made Olingah feel embarrassed. He turned around and stuck out his tongue at them. But this just made them laugh more. Olingah sat down lower on his seat. His eyes filled with tears. Leezah put her arm around him. "Just ignore them," she said. The children kept teasing for a while but eventually they lost interest.

As the bus drove along the dirt road it dropped children off at their farms along the way. The Fitzgeralds' farm was the last one and the bus was empty of children, and quiet, as they said good afternoon to Ms Rowbottom and stepped out. "Bye," said Ms Rowbottom and closed the bus door with the leaver near the steering wheel. The school bus turned around at the gate and drove back off down the road in a whirling cloud of dust.

Feeding out

The front gate creaked on its hinges as the children came in. They went around the back of the farmhouse and up the steps to the verandah. They hung up their coats and school bags. They put away their school shoes, ready for the next school day. Then they washed their hands at the toilet just off the verandah before going in to the kitchen.

"Hi my loves," called Daddy drying his hands and giving his children big hugs. "How was your day at school?"

On the kitchen table were three glasses of juice, some sliced up fruit and some muesli bars. The children were hungry and sat up to eat their snack.

"My day was good," said Skye. "We're going to do a Christmas play Daddy and I am going to be Mary! Everyone wants to be Mary and Mr Lees said I can be Mary!! I get to wear a white dress and a blue headscarf. That's how you know I'm Mary. Everyone else wears brown. And Zoe is going to be one of the three wise men." Zoe was Skye's best friend from school. Zoe lived in town.

"Wonderful Skye! I'm sure you'll be a great Mary. We just need to take the Skye out of your name and you are Mary!" joked Daddy.

Skye giggled.

"What about you possum?" Daddy asked Olingah, stroking his cheek. "You look tired my boy?"

Olingah looked at his Daddy and his eyes filled with tears again. "The big kids teased me Daddy. I hate the big kids. They're so mean." Daddy raised his eyebrows as if to say, "What happened?" So Leezah explained.

"It sounds like you felt really embarrassed." said Dad.

"I don't want to catch the bus anymore Daddy," said Olingah sadly, chewing on his muesli bar. "I think I'll just stay home from now on."

"Okay possum. No more school buses for Olly. But how about you come give me a big hug. And then I'll tell you a story while we go to feed out. I know a good story about Someone Who used to get teased by some meanies."

After their snack the children changed out of their school uniforms and into their farm clothes. They pulled on their boots and went around to the front of the house where the white Ute was parked. The children climbed on the back. They held tight to the bar behind the cabin. Daddy drove across to the paddocks to the haybarn. The haybarn was a huge shed full of big rectangular bales of hay. The children loved to play there in the weekends, making tunnels in the hay. But during the week it was a place of work.

Daddy backed the Ute up against the hay bales. He climbed up on the back of the Ute. The children climbed out of the Ute and up to the top of the haystack. One at a time they pushed the bales down to Daddy who stacked them on the back of the Ute. When the Ute was full of hay the children jumped off the haystack onto the back of the Ute. They held on again to the bar behind the cabin. Daddy started the engine and drove back across the paddocks. Just before he got to the farmhouse he turned right and stopped. Skye jumped off the back and opened the gate. The Ute drove through. Skye shut the gate and clambered back on.

Daddy drove across the little creek and up the hill to the paddock behind the little forest of gum trees. In the paddock were 150 cows. Daddy started to drive very slowly. Leezah pulled her pocketknife out of her pocket and cut the strings tied around the bales of hay. Olingah and Skye pushed the dusty hay off the back of the Ute. It fell in chunks to the ground As Daddy drove slowly along they left a trail of hay across the paddock. The cows gathered around. Some of the cows started eating the hay that the children had pushed onto the ground for them. But some of them were greedy. They wanted the big bales of hay that were on the back of the Ute.

One cow stuck her head over the side of the Ute and started tugging at the hay.

"Hey!" shouted Leezah, "we haven't cut the string on that one yet!" She tried to push the cow's head away from the Ute. But the cow gently butted Leezah with her head and continued to follow the Ute along, pulling at the hay. "Hey!" said the children, laughing.

They all tried to push the cow away from the hay. But she was very determined. Leezah cut the string from the bale and they pushed it over the side of the Ute to the cow. She stopped following the Ute to eat her big pile of hay. "She could put a sticker next to Determination on the virtues chart," giggled Olingah.

When all the cows had been fed and all the hay had been tossed off the back of the Ute, Daddy drove back to the shed. He parked the white Ute next to the orange Ute. "Mum's home," said Dad. Skye gathered up the strings from the hay bales and put them in the incinerator. It was very important to make sure none of the strings got pushed off the Ute with the hay. It could make the cows very sick if they accidentally ate a string.

Olingah swept the hay off the back of the Ute and Leezah fed the dogs their evening meal. By the time they finished it was getting dark. Lights shone from the farmhouse. The girls raced each other down the slope from the shed to the house. Olingah walked behind with his Dad. They stopped at the hen house to lock the door.

"You didn't tell me the story yet Dad," Olingah reminded his father.

"How about we make it the bedtime story?" he suggested.

"Alrighty," said Olingah.

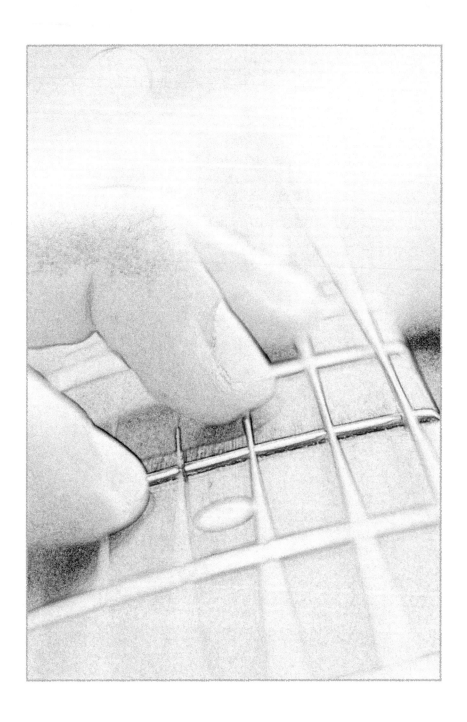

Evening at Fellowship Farm

Leezah and Skye-Maree ran up the back steps and tossed off their boots. They ran to their mother and threw their arms around her waist. Each one yelled: "I WIN!"

Mummy hugged her rowdy girls and then said two words: "Boots! Orderliness!" The girls went back out to the verandah and put their boots away.

"What's for dinner mum?" they called from the verandah.

"Dry bread and mouldy cheese," their mum called back. That was what their mum always said. They knew it wasn't true.

"Can we help?"

"Yes you can. First of all you can both put a sticker on the virtues chart for helpfulness. Then Skye can set the table and Leezah can make a salad," their mum said, turning the chops over on the grill.

Soon dinner was ready and the Fitzgerald family sat down to eat. They shared their news from their day. Dr Fitzgerald talked about a baby hawk that was brought in to the surgery with a damaged wing and a dog that had been hit by a car. Dr Fitzgerald had stitched up the dog and she said it would soon be fine.

Leezah loved animals. But she knew she could never be a vet. She couldn't bear to see animals sick or in pain. When she saw a wounded animal she felt like she herself was wounded. Her mum only told stories about animals that she had been able to help, so that Leezah wouldn't get sad.

It was Daddy and Skye's turn to wash up after dinner. Olingah, Leezah and Mummy went to have showers and brush their teeth. Skye put on the yellow rubber gloves and filled the sink with hot bubbly water. Even the smallest gloves in the supermarket were way too big for Skye. Her fingers only reached half way up the glove's fingers. But it was better than having her fingers scalded by the hot water.

Skye washed and Daddy dried and put the dishes away. And while they cleaned up they listened to Red Grammer. "I think you're wonderful," Skye sang along with the C.D.,

"When somebody says that to me, I feel wonderful, as wonderful can be."

"It makes me want to say," Daddy sang along, "the same thing to somebody new. And by the way, I've been meaning to say: I think you're wonderful too." Daddy bumped his hip against Skye and Skye bumped him back.

When the dishes were clean Skye and Daddy had their showers. Then when everyone was clean and bundled up in their pajamas and dressing gowns, they came and sat by the fire for evening prayers. Daddy had cut his fingers when he was fixing the fences that morning so he passed the guitar to Mummy. Mummy started to strum a melody they all knew well. "Blessed is the spot, and the house, and the place, and the city, and the heart, and the mountain," they all sang, "and the refuge, and the cave, and the valley and the land, and the sea, and the island and the meadow, where mention of God hath been made, and His praise glorified. Bahá'u'lláh," they finished the prayer.

They sang and read prayers together until Olingah's eyes started to close. Then Mummy put away the guitar and Daddy led Olingah off to bed. "Don't forget you promised to tell me a story," said Olingah, in a sleepy voice. "Of course I won't forget," Daddy assured him.

Olingah climbed into bed and the girls and Daddy sat near him. Mummy came in and kissed her tired boy good night. She turned on the nightlight and turned off the overhead light. "You girls come and do your homework when the story's finished, okay?"

"Yes Mummy," said Leezah and Skye. Mummy went back to the living room to read. Daddy started to tell the story he promised Olingah.

The story of the One Who was teased

From the age of nine until He was an old man 'Abdu'l-Bahá lived as a prisoner. Each time He was sent to a new city as a prisoner He would shower His love on all the people around Him and eventually a lot of them realized that He was a very wonderful Man, not a bad person.

When He was living in Akka some of 'Abdu'l-Bahá's enemies stirred up lots of trouble. A group of people came from another city just so that they could be mean to 'Abdu'l-Bahá. They said He was a bad person. They said they were going to kill Him.

'Abdu'l-Bahá always spoke to them with courtesy and calmness. He never got angry and He was never rude. When they asked Him silly questions He was patient. And when they said bad things about Him He just turned His heart toward God.

But all the people around 'Abdu'l-Bahá were scared. Even the people 'Abdu'l-Bahá had helped so much were scared to come to Him to ask for help. The Bahá'ís were very worried that these mean people were going to take 'Abdu'l-Bahá away and hurt Him.

One day a kind man came to 'Abdu'l-Bahá and said: "I have a boat. I can take You away from these mean people who say awful things about You. I can take You to a safe place where no-one will hurt You." The Bahá'ís wanted to protect 'Abdu'l-Bahá. They said: "'Abdu'l-Bahá, You should go with this man"

'Abdu'l-Bahá told the friends that the Báb and Bahá'u'lláh had never run away from Their difficulties. He said that He would follow their example and not run away. He would be courageous and detached.

So 'Abdu'l-Bahá did not run away. Instead He did all the helpful things that He usually did. He mended the house. He planted trees in His garden. He bought some coal for the winter.

The mean people kept saying awful things to 'Abdu'l-Bahá. They sent a boat to take 'Abdu'l-Bahá away. The boat came closer and closer. But 'Abdu'l-Bahá wasn't scared. He put all His trust in God. He prayed and then He waited patiently.

Suddenly the boat turned around and went back out to sea. It returned to the land it had come from and it never came back. So God protected 'Abdu'l-Bahá. And 'Abdu'l-Bahá showed everyone that no matter how mean people are, if we are courteous, and calm, and we pray and trust in God, everything will work out okay.

Monsters in the boot room

Olingah just managed to stay awake for the whole story. When it was over he murmured a sleepy good night and slid under his covers. Leezah, Skye and Daddy kissed him good night and went quietly back out to the living room.

Olingah's bedtime was 7 o'clock. Skye was allowed to stay up until 8 o'clock and Leezah's bedtime was half an hour after Skye. Skye didn't always have homework so she often spent the hour reading and drawing. Skye got her felt pens from the art cupboard, a book to lean on and some scrap paper. She sat down on the rug in front of the fire to draw. Leezah went out to her school bag to get her homework.

It was dark out in the Boot Room – where they kept their coats and bags and boots. She walked toward her bag. Suddenly she saw two bright yellow eyes shining in the darkness. She heard a screeching sound.

Leezah leaped backward and screamed.

Mummy, Daddy and Skye came running through the kitchen and out the back door into the Boot Room. Leezah clutched her Dad and pointed to where she had seen the yellow eyes.

Just then, the terrified possum who had been in Leezah's school bag scrambled across the floorboards and shot up a nearby tree. Leezah started to laugh. Mummy pulled an apple core and a half eaten sandwich out of Leezah's bag. "We have had a visit from an apple-core thief," she said. "Caught in the act!"

"I think Leezah's scream was enough punishment for any thief," said Daddy putting his arm around his daughter's shoulders as they went inside.

Mummy emptied Leezah's lunchbox and rinsed it. Leezah gathered her schoolbooks and went to sit at the table behind the couch. Daddy sat down on the couch and propped his feet on Skye's back. "Aah the perfect foot rest, " he said and closed his eyes.

"Daaaad!" said Skye and sat up straight so his feet fell to the floor.

"Oh sorry Skye, was that you?" Dad asked, winking.

Leezah was working on a project she was doing for school. Everyone in the class could choose an animal to study. Leezah knew straight away what she would choose. Dogs. She loved dogs. Tonight Leezah was working on her drawing of four newborn puppies drinking milk from the bitch –the mother dog. She imagined what it would be like to have a puppy of her very own.

She and Skye and Olingah sometimes pretended that they each had a little puppy. When they did their work on the farm they would call their pretend puppies. They rolled in the grass letting their pretend puppies lick their faces. And when their imaginary puppies were naughty they would gently scold them.

But it wasn't the same as having a real puppy. There were dogs on the farm but they were working dogs. They were trained to round up the cows. They weren't cute and cuddly. And the children weren't allowed to play with the working dogs anyway.

When Leezah finished her drawing she took it out to show her mum. Mummy had just finished making the school lunches. She was putting the kettle on for a cup of tea.

"Darling, what a lovely picture. It's beautiful. Well done," she said as Leezah held up her project book. Then Leezah put her books and pens in her school bag. She came back into the kitchen and pushed herself up to sit on the kitchen table.

"Mum," said Leezah.

"Yes doll," said her Mum reaching into the fridge for the milk.

"Can I pleeeease have one."

"One what?" her mum asked.

"You know."

"One kiss?" Mummy teased, kissing Leezah's forehead.

"No Mum!"

Leezah's mum looked at her. They had had this conversation many many times.

"You said I could have one when I'm older, and now I'm older! I'll be responsible, I promise."

"We'll see," said Mum. It was the worst answer. Leezah felt very frustrated.

"Pleeease Mum?"

"Leezah," said Mum. Leezah knew there was no point in talking about it any more. She had been asking for a pet puppy all year.

She knew she could take care of a puppy. What was so hard about it? You feed it. You give it water. You brush it, wash it, play with it. You walk it and train it to be obedient. And you run with it on the beach, and snuggle with it and...it felt so unfair.

Skye brought her artwork out to the kitchen. She had also been drawing puppies. Five fat puppies, all different colors. She gave it to her mum and kissed her goodnight.

Daddy was already asleep on the couch but she kissed him too and then went off to bed. Leezah sat with her Mummy reading for another half an hour. Just before bedtime she sat on the floor in front of Mummy's armchair. Mummy brushed Leezah's thick black hair and plaited it into two long plaits. Leezah kissed her mummy and her sleeping daddy and went off to bed.

She climbed the creaky bunk ladder and crawled under her covers. "Yá Bahá'u'l-Abhá" she whispered and closed her eyes. That night Leezah dreamt that her picture came to life and she had four little puppies to care for.

Goodnight from the Fitzgeralds

Mummy locked the back door and turned on the outside light. In the living room Daddy was fast asleep on the couch. He got up even earlier than the rest of them so by early evening he always fell asleep. His book was resting on his tummy. Mummy made sure the fire was safely out and put up the fire screen. Then she woke the sleeping daddy and he wandered off to bed.

After she had brushed her teeth Mummy went in to check on the sleeping children. Skye, as always had kicked her entire quilt onto the floor. Mummy picked it up and spread it over her eight-year-old daughter. Leezah lay flat on her back with her arms stretched up past her ears. Olingah was snuggled under his pillow and blanket, with just his nose sticking out for air. Because of the way he slept his sisters sometimes called him wombat. He was like a little wombat deep in his burrow.

Mummy pulled open the bedroom curtains to let in the night breeze. The breeze brought the smell of the sea, which was not far away. The stars were very bright in the clear sky. Outside in the garden the nighttime animals were having their usual sing along, with crickets chirping, owls hooting, and possums screeching.

As she turned to leave the room Leezah stirred. "Mummy," she whispered sleepily, "I'm thirsty." Mummy went to the kitchen and brought Leezah back a drink bottle with some water from the tap. Leezah drank some and gave the bottle back to her mum who put it on the little table between the bunk bed and Olingah's bed. "Mummy," Leezah said, dangling her arm over the side of the bed, "Can you come snuggle with me, just for a minute."

Mummy stroked Leezah's arm and gently pushed it back onto the bed. She climbed slowly up the ladder and stretched out next to her eldest daughter. Mummy's long legs poked through the bars at the end of the bed. "You go to sleep now," she said to Leezah. Leezah closed her eyes and Mummy lay next to her, stroking her forehead. When Leezah had fallen back to sleep Mummy slowly sat up and slipped quietly down the bunk ladder.

Out in the hallway she turned on the lamp so that anyone needing the toilet in the night would be able to see. Then she joined Daddy in their bed. As she lay down to sleep she also whispered: "Yá Bahá'u'l-Abhá" and soon all the Fitzgeralds of Fellowship Farm were fast asleep.

As they lay sleeping none of them could have guessed what a surprise the next day was going to bring. But that is another story ...

BOOK TWO

FLEA, FLEX & FIZZ

Leezah, Skye-Maree, and Olingah Fitzgerald of Fellowship Farm love puppies. They do school projects on puppies. They draw them, they dream about them and they beg their parents to let them have a puppy of their own.

But their mummy and daddy say it's not the right time.

Then one day, coming home from school, they find something unusual by the side of the road, that might just turn out to be the answer to their prayers...

A mysterious moving sack

It was the end of the school day. Most of the children lived in the township so they walked home or rode their bikes or got picked up. But Leezah and some of the other children at Kellyton Primary lived on farms some distance from the school. They went home each day on the school bus driven by Ms Rowbottom.

So Leezah and the other children in grade five said goodbye to their teacher Mr Dunlop, collected their bags from the coatroom and went to wait for the bus. When Leezah arrived at the big oak tree, her little sister and brother were already there, waiting for the bus doors to open.

"Hi Skye! Hi Olly!" Leezah greeted them.

"Hi Leezah!" They both said together, turning to face their sister and grinning.

Skye's yellow school skivvy was covered with blood stains.

"What's that?" asked Leezah, pointing to the stains.

"I got a bleeding nose," said Skye. "I was just about to kick a goal and then Joana came charging at me and ended up falling on top of me and we clunked heads."

"Oh Skye," said Leezah giving her a hug. Skye-Maree was eight, and in grade three. She was very tall for her age. And very strong. She loved sport, especially football. And so she often came home bandaged or bloodstained!

"Look what I made!" said Olingah proudly, holding out a juice bottle that had been turned into bright green pig. Olingah was six and was just finishing his first year of school. He was so happy to be going to school with his older sisters at last.

"Good Job Olly!" said Leezah admiring the bright green pig.

It was 3:15pm so Ms Rowbottom opened the doors of the red school bus to let the children on. While they waited in line to get on, some of the children wrote their names in the dust covering the old bus.

"Hey I just remembered you said yesterday you weren't going to catch the bus anymore Olly. Because the big kids teased you."

"Never mind about the teasing," said Olly trying to be brave as he stepped up into the bus. "'Abdu'l-Bahá had worse teasing and He didn't run away."

But as it turned out Olly didn't need to be brave that day. As Skye stepped into the bus after Olingah, an orange Ute pulled into the school grounds and honked. It was Dr Fitzgerald - Leezah, Skye and Olingah's mum.

Olingah caught sight of his mum from inside the bus. "Hey that's my mum! Mummy!" he called excitedly clambering out of the bus. Mocking voices followed him calling "Muuummy Muuumy". Olingah didn't even notice. He jumped off the last step and ran to the car. He scrambled in.

Leezah and Skye went to their mum's window. "Hi Mum," they said. "Are you going home early today?" Dr Fitzgerald usually worked each afternoon as the town vet and got home after the children, at 5 o'clock.

"Yes. No sick animals this afternoon, so I can give you all a ride home," she smiled.

The girls threw their bags into the back of the Ute and climbed in behind Dr Fitzgerald.

Dr Fitzgerald drove out of the school yard and through the town. When she reached the dirt road that led to the farms she turned right. The children chatted with their mother about their day at school and Olly showed his mum the bright green pig he had made.

Soon the Fitzgerald family farm could be seen off in the distance – Fellowship Farm. Suddenly Skye, who was in the backseat with Leezah cried out: "Oh look! A wombat!"

"Where?" asked Olly straining against his seatbelt to see out the window.

"On the side of the road!"

Dr Fitzgerald slowed the car to a stop. They clambered out of the car and walked slowly back along the road to where Skye had seen the wombat.

When they got close they realized that Skye hadn't seen a wombat at all. It was a brown hessian sack. And something inside was moving.

Inside the sack

As soon as Dr Fitzgerald saw the bag she knew what it was. It was tied tightly shut with strong string. None of them had their pocket knives with them.

"Get back into the car please," she said to Leezah, Skye and Olingah. Dr Fitzgerald picked up the bag and as she did whatever was inside started thrashing back and forth and yelping. She carried the bag to the back of the Ute and started the car.

"What is it Mummy? What's in the bag? Is it a monster?" asked Olingah.

"No honey it's not a monster," said his mum.

As they drove the rest of the way home Dr Fitzgerald explained what was in the bag. She told them that sometimes people let their pets have babies but then the people don't know what to do with the babies. They might try and find homes for them but if no-one wants the puppies or kittens, sometimes the owners just get rid of them. Dr Fitzgerald explained that inside the bag were abandoned puppies.

Nobody wanted to take care of the puppies so the owners just left them in a bag to die. Leezah's eyes filled with tears. She couldn't think of anything more cruel. Leezah loved animals, especially puppies. And it made her very very sad to think of them being hurt.

When they got home Skye ran into the kitchen to get scissors to cut the tough yarn that held the bag shut. Usually when they got home their Daddy was there to meet them from the bus. But Dr Fitzgerald had called him to let him know he could stay out on the farm and keep working. She was bringing the children home and would get their afternoon snack today. Skye ran back with the scissors. Dr Fitzgerald lowered the sack to the ground and carefully cut it open.

Inside the sack were four little puppies. They were all colored white and brown and black. They were dusty and weak and scared. Leezah ran to the back of the house, up the stairs and into the kitchen. She grabbed the milk from the fridge and a dish from the cupboard. She raced back to the front of the house. Three of the puppies were timidly exploring the nearby grass and plants. But one little puppy just lay on its side, panting.

Dr Fitzgerald saw Leezah bringing the dish and the milk. "Good girl darling," she said. "That was helpful and considerate." Leezah poured the milk into the dish and the children gently nudged the puppies toward it. The puppies had not really learned how to drink from a dish but they were so thirsty that they did their best to slurp up the milk.

Leezah dipped her finger in the milk and dropped some drops of it into the sick puppy's mouth. Its eyes were closed and it was breathing very quickly. "Let's take them all around the back," suggested Dr Fitzgerald. Each of the children took a puppy and Dr Fitzgerald gently carried the sick one and the milk dish.

The children helped their mother make a little bed for the sick puppy. They used an old woolen jumper that didn't fit Olingah anymore. They made the bed on the verandah and lay the sick puppy on it. Meanwhile, the other three puppies drank some more milk and started to totter around. Their little pink tongues hung from the mouths. Their noses and whiskers were covered in milk. They sniffed the grass and the stairs and each other. Every now and then one or the other would sit down and scratch, or make a little whining noise. The children lay down on the grass near the puppies. The puppies sniffed their faces. "Yuck!" said Skye, wiping milk and puppy saliva from her nose.

Dr Fitzgerald went into the kitchen. She reached up to a top cupboard and pulled down a box full of medicines, syringes, bandages and other things. She filled a needle with some medicine and went out to the sick puppy. She pulled up a fold of skin and stuck the needle in. The puppy was too sick to even notice.

"Is it going to be alright Mum?" Leezah asked while a puppy slobbered in her ear.

"I don't know," said Mum looking worried.

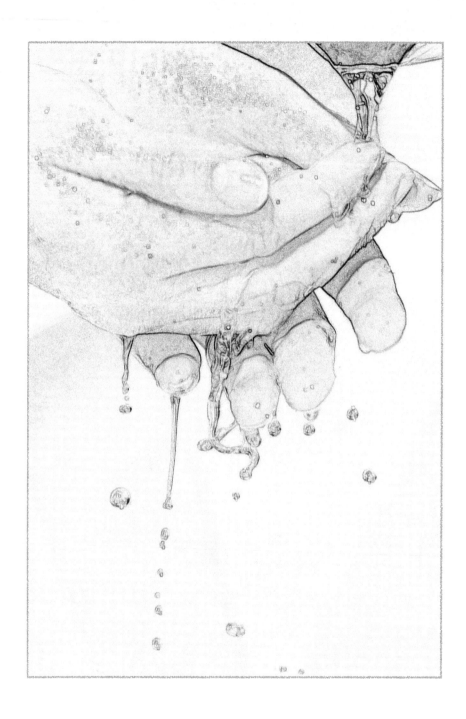

Skye's sacrifice

When Dr Fitzgerald had attended to the sick puppy she went into the kitchen and washed her hands. As she cut up fruit for the children's snack she called to them: "I want you all to wash your hands and come have your snack now please."

No-one was hungry but they obeyed their mum. They took off their coats and shoes in the boot room, washed their hands at the outside toilet and went into the kitchen. Mummy gave them the cut up fruit, poured some juice and handed out muesli bars. While the children ate they could hear the puppies rustling around and gently whining every now and then.

They all wanted to be with the puppies but, like every afternoon, there was work on the farm to be done after snack. Daddy would come to the house at 4:30 to take the children to feed the cows. After their snack the children went to change from their school uniforms into their farm clothes. While they were changing Skye started to think of something generous to do for her brother and sister.

Skye really wanted to stay and play with the puppies. And she knew Leezah and Olingah did too. So she said: "If Daddy says its okay, I don't mind feeding out by myself today. You two can stay with the puppies." Leezah and Olingah's faces lit up! They gave Skye a big hug and rushed out to the kitchen. Leezah grabbed the farm radio: "Base to mobile one, over," she said excitedly. This was how she called her daddy by radio. She heard her daddy's voice answer "Mobile one to base, over."

Leezah quickly told her dad about the puppies and about Skye's offer to do the feeding out by herself if Daddy agreed. "Okay," agreed Dad. "Tell Skye I'll be there to pick her up in five minutes. Over and out."

Skye came into the kitchen pulling her farm jumper over her head. Her mum gave her a big hug that lifted Skye off her feet. "That was very generous of you Skye. Why don't you put a sticker on the virtues chart." Skye chose a clown sticker and put it on the family virtues chart next to the word Generous. The chart was a big piece of cardboard with all the virtues written on it. Each time one of them was generous, or patient, or helpful, or obedient, or courageous, or some other virtue, they could add a sticker to the chart. They were trying to get the Fitzgerald Family Virtues chart all full of stickers, by practicing the virtues.

Daddy pulled up in the white Ute out the front of the house and honked on the horn. Skye ran out the back, gave the puppies a little stroke and kept going round to the front. She jumped on the back of the Ute and held on tight to the bar. Mr Fitzgerald drove to the haybarn. Skye helped him push the hay onto the back of the Ute and then they drove to the paddock where the cows were. As Mr Fitzgerald drove slowly along, Skye cut the strings and pushed the hay off. Usually the children all did it together and it was much faster. But Skye did her best and soon all the hay had been fed out to the cows.

They drove back to the shed, swept the hay off the Ute, and fed the dogs. Then they locked up the chickens and went back to the farmhouse just as the sun was setting. As the sun set the air grew very cool. Even though it was the end of spring, it was still cool in Tasmania. Skye slipped her smooth strong hand into her dad's rough strong hand. She talked about the puppies they had found. "Do you think we can keep them?" she asked her dad.

Mr Fitzgerald just chuckled and said: "We'll see."

When they arrived the lights were shining from the windows and the smell of baking vegetables was wafting from the kitchen. They walked around the back. The puppies were nowhere to be seen. As they went into the boot room however they saw three little puppies snuggled up in an old horse rug, fast asleep. Mr Fitzgerald and Skye quietly took off their boots and went inside.

In the kitchen it was very quiet. Leezah was setting the table and Olingah was pouring five cups of juice. Olingah's eyes were red and tears streamed down Leezah's face as she did her work.

"What happened?" asked Skye-Maree.

A funeral

Dr Fitzgerald pulled the hot tray of vegetables and tofu from the oven and put it on the sink. She dished some onto each plate. As she put the plates on the table and slid the vegetable tray into the sink to soak, she answered Skye: "We have some sad news Skye...The puppy that was sick has died."

"Oh," said Skye quietly. "Where is it?"

Dr Fitzgerald explained that they had wrapped it up and put it in the outside fridge. Tomorrow the children could bury it in the garden.

"Are the others okay?" Skye asked

"Yes, they have had some milk and a play and now they are sleeping... Let's all have some dinner now," suggested Dr Fitzgerald.

The family sat up to eat. At first it was unusually quiet. Then Olingah started to ask some questions. "Mum, does the puppy have a soul?"

"No, honey, not like humans have souls."

"Does it have a puppy soul?"

"Not really. It has a spirit that exists while its body is alive. But then when its body dies, the spirit goes too."

"So where is the puppy now?"

"Well..." Dr Fitzgerald paused. "The body of the puppy is in the outside fridge. But the spirit is gone."

"But where did it go Mum?" Olingah persisted.

Leezah helped him to understand. She told him that it was just like when Olingah made a car out of Lego. When you put all the blocks together and add the wheels and the little plastic steering wheel, you have a Lego car. But if you take the blocks apart and the wheels off, you don't have a Lego car anymore. But the car hasn't gone anywhere. It just doesn't exist anymore. Olingah looked a bit confused but he didn't ask any more questions.

After dinner the washing up was done, showers were had and prayers were sung. At seven o'clock – Olingah's bedtime - Dr Fitzgerald told them a bedtime story. The children loved her stories. Usually they were about three children called Leezah, Skye-Maree and Olingah. The children in her stories had all sorts of adventures, like flying helicopters by themselves, diving under the ocean, finding secret tunnels, and shrinking to the size of caterpillar. After the story, Olingah went to sleep while Skye and Leezah did their homework. By 8:30 all the children were in bed and close to being asleep.

The following morning they woke up even earlier than usual so that they would have time to bury the puppy before going to school. After prayers and breakfast they divided up the morning chores. They liked to do them together but it took longer that way.

When all the farm animals were fed the children met back at the farmhouse. Skye took a shovel and dug a hole at the end of the garden underneath her dad's rose bushes.

Leezah carefully took the plastic bag with the puppy in it from the outside fridge. The children carried it to the hole and slowly took the plastic bag off. They placed the puppy in the hole and covered it gently with dirt.

Then each of the children gathered daisies, daffodils and jonquils and put them on top of the place where the puppy had been buried. They didn't know what to do next so they decided to sing a little prayer that they knew about animals, from 'Abdu'l-Bahá. They held hands and sang:

"If an animal be sick let the children try to heal it, if it be hungry let them feed it. If it be thirsty let them quench its thirst. If it be weary let them see that it rests." They all felt a little bit sad. They had tried to heal the sick animal, but they hadn't succeeded.

It was time to pack their bags and go wait for the school bus. The puppy's grave looked beautiful with the spring flowers on top. They looked at it for a second more and then turned and went up to the house to get ready for school.

A treasure hunt

That afternoon after school as the children came home on the bus they talked about the puppies. They all really wanted to keep the puppies. But Leezah had been asking for a puppy all year and her parents had not agreed.

"What will Mum and Dad do with them then?" asked Skye

"I don't know, maybe find homes for them," said Leezah quietly.

"Well let's play with them all weekend at least," said Olingah. They all thought their parents would at least let them keep the puppies for the weekend.

The bus pulled up at Fellowship Farm and the Fitzgeralds got off. "Bye Ms Rowbottom," they called as she closed the doors, turned the bus around and drove back down the long dusty road to the town. The children hurried to the back of the house to find the puppies. But the puppies were not in the yard and they were not in the boot room. They quickly took off their coats and shoes and washed their hands. Then they went into the kitchen.

Usually their Dad was there making their snack when they got home from school. But the kitchen was empty. On the table was a note.

Leezah quickly read the note then she smiled and said: "Yay! A treasure hunt."

Sometimes on weekends the Fitzgerald family played a game called treasure hunt. One of the adults would write a series of notes and hide them in different places. The children had to follow the clue on each note to find the next note. When they got to the last note there was usually a little special treat for each of them. It was one of their favorite games.

Skye read the note aloud:

In a house that's quite absurd
There's not one person
Only birds.

The children rushed off to the pigeon house. Their Daddy had a big cage full of pigeons that he had trained to fly out around the farm and come back. Sure enough on the door of the pigeon house there was another note:

Go to a gate that's big and blue,
If you want another clue.

The children left the pigeon house and ran off to the front gate of the farm. They had been in such a rush when they came home that they had not noticed a small piece of paper tucked into the wooden rails of the gate.

In this place there's a green toy
That's cuddled by a little boy

"My bed!" cried Olingah. "My green rabbit is the toy, and I'm the little boy!!" The children ran back around the house to the back verandah. Boots went flying in all directions and even Olingah's tight boots got yanked off in seconds. There in the bed was the next clue:

Have a look if you are able
Underneath the kitchen table!

"We're right back where we started," laughed Leezah as the children ran to the kitchen and dropped to the floor. A note was stuck under the table. Leezah pulled it off and they sat on the floor to read it.

Change your clothes from school to play
Go to where there's lots of hay

The children rushed to their bedroom and threw off their school uniforms. Blue pants, white socks, yellow skivvies went flying in all directions. Orderliness was completely forgotten. Even Skye's precious Mary costume with the white dress and blue head scarf that was hanging proudly on a coat hanger on the outside of the cupboard got pushed hastily aside in the rush to find socks and jumpers, skivvies and pants. They pulled on their farm clothes and hurried out of the house and the yard.

The haybarn was about half a kilometer from the farmhouse. Usually they drove in the Ute with their dad. But no-one was tired. They were all excited to find out what might be at the end of the treasure hunt.

When they arrived at the barn they found an arrow made of sticks pointing to the top of the haystack.

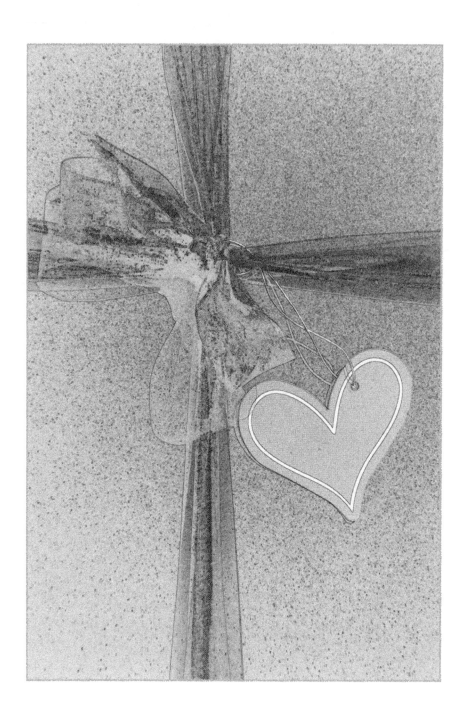

A parcel of joy

The children often spent many hours in the haybarn making tunnels in the hay. But today they were focused on something else. They helped each other to climb the slippery hay to the top of the stack. When they got there they knew they had come to the end of treasure hunt. There were three small parcels there, wrapped in red wrapping paper.

"What could it be?" asked Olingah as they each took a parcel and began to pull the paper off. Inside each package was something that made each of the children open their eyes wide. They couldn't believe what they saw. Just then they heard the Ute pull up to the haybarn. They grabbed their gifts and scrambled down the hay.

Their dad stepped out of the Ute, smiling. "I guess you must be hungry. No snack today!"

"No!! We're not hungry! Daddy, do these mean what we think they mean?" asked Leezah with excitement. Each of the children had unwrapped their gift to find a little leather collar and a dog leash. "Can we keep the puppies?"

Daddy smiled at his children and winked. Then he slowly nodded his head. "Hooray hooray hooray" the children all screamed out and jumped up and down, hugging each other.

Just then three furry little faces appeared at window from inside the Ute. The puppies wanted to know what all the fuss was about. Each of the children gently pulled a puppy through the window of the Ute and snuggled it to themselves. Then the children helped each other put the little leather collars around the necks of the wiggling, sniffing, licking puppies.

"Okay my darlings," said Daddy eventually. "Don't forget we have some hungry cows to feed," said Dad.

"Okay Daddy," they said. Each of them put their puppy back in the cabin of the Ute. They put their leashes in too. Then they clambered up the hay to push it down on to the back of the Ute.

• •

That evening as the children went to bed they took some time to settle. They thought of their puppies sleeping in the basket in the boot room and waves of joy rippled over them. Long after lights out, even Olingah lay awake whispering with his sisters about all the wonderful things they planned to do with their very own puppies.

The next morning the children got up as usual at six o'clock. After morning prayers, breakfast and farm chores, they still had some time to play with their puppies. They lay down on the damp grass and let the puppies climb on them, tickling their faces with their little pink tongues.

When Mummy came to call them to get ready for school, they asked: "Can we pleeease take them to school Mum?" Mummy just laughed and went back into the kitchen. The children hurried to get ready for school then had a few more minutes with their puppies until the school bus came.

As they rode to school they talked about what names they would give to their dogs. Leezah and Olingah's puppies were girls and Skye's was a boy.

"I'm going to call my puppy Flea," announced Olingah in the end. Leezah and Skye thought that it was a funny name for a dog. But they knew Olingah was being serious and they knew how awful it felt to be laughed at. So they didn't laugh.

"Okay Olly. But if you call her Flea, maybe she'll get fleas?" said Skye.

"No, Skye," said Olly in a patient, grown-up voice. "She can't get fleas from her name. Just from other dogs."

"True," agreed Skye.

Skye thought of different names that she liked. Then she thought of the virtues chart in the kitchen with all its bright stickers on it. "I know," she said. "I'm going to call my puppy Flexibility."

"Flexibility?" queried Leezah

"Yup. Flexibility." Skye liked the sound of that word. It was the perfect name for her puppy.

"Okay, so we've got Flea Fitzgerald and Flexibility Fitzgerald," observed Leezah. "Maybe I should choose a name starting with 'F' too." Skye and Olingah had lots of suggestions. But in the end Leezah decided to call her puppy Firefly... Fizz for short.

To the doghouse

The last days of spring passed quickly. The children were busy with their school activities, their work on the farm and most of all with their new puppies, Flea, Flexibility (Flex), and Firefly (Fizz). The puppies grew bigger and stronger and some changes had to be made.

"Oh no!" cried Leezah one morning when she came to let them out of the boot room and give them their morning milk. Her blue leather school shoes had been chewed up and there was a big pooh on Skye's gumboot.

"I think its time these puppies moved out of the boot room," said Mr Fitzgerald. "We'll have to make the fence around the back garden more secure and make a kennel for them," he added.

So when the weekend came the Fitzgerald family got to work. Leezah, Skye and Mr Fitzgerald fixed all the holes in the garden fence so that no little puppies could sneak out. Olingah and Dr Fitzgerald sawed the wood and started to hammer it together to make a doghouse big enough for three fully grown dogs. When the doghouse was finished they all helped to paint it. On the roof of the kennel the children painted the names of their puppies and big black puppy paw prints.

The doghouse looked great. For a full day they left it to dry. Then on Sunday afternoon they let the puppies loose in the yard to explore their new territory and house. The children took the old horse blanket from the puppies' basket in the boot room, and put it inside doghouse so the puppies would feel at home.

The puppies explored the big stretch of grass, the flower beds, the fence and the doghouse. It was all very interesting and they sniffed and panted, wiggled and tumbled around the garden for the whole afternoon. The children followed them, tickling, chasing and tumbling along beside them. When evening came the children took the puppies to the doghouse and put them inside. The puppies came straight out and followed the children across the lawn. They tried to climb the steps leading up to the verandah and the boot room.

"No Flex!" said Skye. "Your bed is over there now." The children carried their puppies back to the doghouse and put them back inside. Then the children sprinted across the lawn and up the steps. But the puppies came running after them.

Daddy had a suggestion: "We might need to tie them to the kennel for the first few nights so they learn that the kennel is their bedroom now." So Mr Fitzgerald hammered a metal stake into the grass in front of the kennel. The children clipped the leashes to the dogs' collars and looped them over the stake. The puppies could go in and out of the kennel but they couldn't go far.

The children cuddled their puppies good night one more time and left them to get used to their new bedroom. As the children crossed the lawn the puppies strained at their leashes, trying desperately to follow them. They whimpered and whined as the children climbed the stairs. When Skye, Leezah and Olingah went inside the kitchen and shut the door Flex, Fizz and Flea began to howl.

Leezah thought her heart was going to break. As the children had their evening prayers, got ready for bed and did their homework, the puppies continued to cry out. Daddy and Mummy said they should just leave them for a night or two and then they will get used to their new home. But the children felt very sad for their lonely puppies as they went off to bed.

At ten o' clock Dr Fitgerald woke her husband who was dozing on the couch and they went to bed. In the children's bedroom there were two little girls lying awake on their beds listening to their puppies. "Leezah, are you awake?" whispered Skye.

"Yep," said Skye's big sister.

"Leezah, I have an idea," said Skye

"What is it?"

Skye told Leezah her idea. It was a crazy one. But in the end they decided to do it. By the time the puppies stopped crying and the girls fell asleep it was very very late and they were exhausted.

The missing children

Olingah woke up and looked at the clock. It was already ten past six. He wondered why Leezah and Skye hadn't woken him up. They always got up at six o'clock. Olingah looked over at Skye's bed. It was empty. He stood up on his bed to look at the top bunk. Leezah's bed was also empty. And the quilt was missing.

Olingah put on his dressing gown and slippers and went looking for his sisters. He checked the bathroom. Not there. He checked the guest room. Not there. He checked the sunroom at the front of the house, the living room and the kitchen. No sisters. Olingah's dad was making the bed in Oinga's parents' room and his mum was lighting the fire and turning on lamps in the living room. But neither of them had seen Leezah or Skye.

"What do you mean they're missing?" asked Mummy.

"They are, " said Olingah. "They're not anywhere."

Mummy went in to the bedroom and turned on the light. No girls. She and Olingah went out to the back verandah. They checked in the boot room full of coats and boots and bags. They checked the outside toilet next to the boot room, with its little stained sink and lots of cobwebs. They checked the laundry at the end of the verandah. But Leezah and Skye were not in any of these places.

Mummy started to get worried. She went to tell Daddy that the girls could not be found. They checked the garden around the house but didn't find a trace of them. They started to call the girls' names: Leezah, Skye, Leezah, Skye.

The calling out woke the puppies and they came out of their kennel to see what was going on. "Hey Flea, Flex, Fizz, " said Olingah. "We've lost Leezah and Skye." The puppies strained at the leashes trying to get to Olingah. They hoped he was going to give them their morning milk. Olingah went back to the kitchen and poured some milk for the puppies. By this time Dr and Mr Fitzgerald were getting really scared. Mr Fitzgerald went up to the shed where the Utes and tractors were kept.

The farm dogs tied to the shed greeted him barking loudly. They were hoping for some breakfast. Dr Fitzgerald went to check the stables. The horses were out in the fields and the stables were empty. She called out: "LEEZAH! SKYE! WHERE ARE YOU?"

Olingah poured the milk into the dish and opened the kitchen door with his foot. But as the door swung open Olingah lost his balance and the dish tipped over, spilling milk all over the floor. "Oh no!" moaned Olingah. He put the dish in the kitchen sink. He rinsed and squeezed the sponge and started to mop up the milk. The milk had splashed all over the floor, the table legs and the cupboards so Olingah had to keep rinsing and squeezing the sponge. Finally the kitchen was more or less clean again.

Olingah took the milk carton and the bowl and carried them down to the doghouse. He set the bowl on ground a little away from the kennel and poured the milk. He could hear his mum and dad walking around the area near the house calling loudly for their missing daughters. Olingah started to feel sick in his tummy from worry.

After he had poured the milk Olingah unclipped the leashes from the collars. The puppies rushed to their breakfast putting their muddy paws in the dish and covering themselves with milk. But as Olingah bent down to unhook the leashes from the stake he saw something very strange.

Inside the doghouse were two big balls covered in a quilt that had waves and fish sewn onto it. "What is Leezah's quilt doing in the doghouse?" Olingah wondered. "And how did those balls get in there?" Olingah reached in and poked the ball nearest to the kennel opening. The ball started to shuffle around and grunt and soon a sleepy face appeared from underneath the quilt.

"Skye?!" exclaimed Olingah.

Dr and Mr Fitzgerald came in the front gate and went down the side of the house toward the backyard. They were frantic with worry. "You call the police," said Mr Fitzgerald. "I'll go get the Ute and check the haybarn." But they didn't need to do either. Because as they rounded the corner of the house, two sleepy girls crawled out of the dog kennel, dragging a quilt behind them. "Morning Mum. Morning Dad," they murmured.

Mary meets Flex

"I found them," called Olingah happily.

Dr and Mr Fitzgerald stopped in their tracks. Their mouths dropped open. They looked at each other. They wanted to laugh and cry at the same time. They wanted to hug their girls and they wanted to scold them. Meanwhile the girls bundled up the quilt and hurried toward the house. The grass was cold on their bare feet and the puppies who had guzzled their milk ran around their ankles, dripping milk and nipping them as they moved.

As they reached the steps their father took the quilt from Leezah and their mother pulled the girls to herself in a tight squeeze. "You are wicked evil and naughty," she scolded, kissing their hair, their ears, their eyes and their noses. "Shall I beat you now or later?" Then she smacked their bottoms playfully and said: "Get inside and get some clothes on before I decide to do it NOW!"

• •

The day at school seemed to last forever for two very tired sisters. That night all three of them went to bed at Olingah's bedtime – 7:30pm. And no-one paid any attention to the miserable puppies crying and calling through the night from their kennel, where they slept all alone. But just as Mummy and Daddy had promised, after three nights in the kennel, the puppies were used to it. They didn't even need to be tied up anymore.

The days passed and soon it was the middle of December and the last day of school for the Fitzgerald children. Their school was doing an end of year concert. All the children were involved. But Skye was especially proud because she had been chosen to play the role of Mary in the grade three Christmas play. On the last day of school Skye put on her white gown and blue headscarf.

"Why do you have to wear that?" asked Olingah.

"Because the Mary in the play ALWAYS wears a blue scarf," said Skye. "That's how you know."

"Know what?" asked Olingah.

"Know that it's Mary. She's the one with the blue scarf, like in all the pictures." Skye pinned her scarf to her hair with brand new ladybird clips.

Leezah and Olingah also dressed for the school concert. Then the children went out the back door to put on their shoes. As Skye-Maree bent over to put her shoes on, Flex and Flea came bounding up the steps. They wagged their tails and slobbered. They wanted to play. Flea bit down on Skye's blue head scarf. She grrrrrred and tugged. The blue headscarf fell from Skye's head, and Flea took off down the steps.

"FLEA!!!" cried Skye, but in her long Mary gown she couldn't run after the puppy.

Leezah and Olingah chased Flea around the garden. Flea dodged this way and that. She ran, dragging the scarf through the flower beds, covering it with saliva and dirt. Finally the children cornered the naughty puppy and rescued the scarf. But it was in filthy tatters. Skye started to cry, as Leezah came up the verandah steps and passed the ripped and dirty headscarf to Skye. "How can I be Mary in this?" she cried.

Mummy came out of the kitchen carrying a tray of fruit for the potluck after the concert. "Don't worry Mary," said Mummy gently. I have an idea.

Mummy took Skye into the house. The others piled into the Ute. Soon Skye and Mummy joined them and they all drove in to the school for the concert.

The adults went and sat in the school hall. The children went backstage to get ready for their performances.

When it was time for the grade three Christmas play, the curtain rose. There in the middle of the stage was a manger with some straw and a doll in it. Next to the manger stood 'Joseph' dressed in brown. On the other side of the manger was Mary, looking lovely in her white gown and beautiful orange headscarf.

BOOK THREE

VISITORS ARRIVE

The school year has just ended for Leezah, Skye-Maree and Olingah of Fellowship Farm. They are very excited about the two months of summer fun stretching ahead.

Then, one morning, they find a letter in the mailbox from their cousins, Nick and Annissa. The letter has some very exciting news, which promises to make the holidays even better than they imagined.

A letter arrives at Fellowship Farm

As the Fitzgerald children finished their morning chores and headed toward the farmhouse they felt very excited. It was the first day of summer holidays. Two months of beaches and sand dunes, fishing and campfires, tunnels in the hay, rope swings in the apple orchard, treehouses, drawing, reading and other wonderful things stretched before them. But best of all, they would be able to spend long hours with their new puppies, Flea, Flex and Fizz.

The puppies were covered in black, brown and white patches. They were only fourteen weeks old. Skye, Leezah and Olingah had found them abandoned in a bag by the side of the road. At first they had been too small to take out of the yard, but now they were getting a little bigger the children could take them across the paddocks on their leashes. When the puppies were a bit bigger the children would start training them, but for now they just used the leashes to stop the puppies getting lost.

Leezah, Skye and Olingah attached the leashes to the leather collars around the puppies' necks and led them out of the back yard.

"Let's walk them over to the dam," suggested Skye.

The dam was in a paddock on the opposite side of the road to the farmhouse. It was safe for the children to cross the road because there were hardly any cars. The Fitzgerald farm was the last farm on the road that came from Kellyton township.

The children opened the big blue gate and crossed the road. The puppies sniffed excitedly and wagged their tails as they explored the new territory. After opening the gate on the other side of the road and closing it behind themselves, the children and their little puppies walked slowly through the grass with the morning sun on their backs.

They walked past the shearing shed and past the pens that held the sheep during the shearing time. Leezah didn't like the shearing.

The shearers seemed to be so rough with the poor sheep. So Skye and Olingah helped in the shearing shed and Leezah helped her dad or mum prepare the food for the shearers. The shearing shed was empty as they went past but there were lols of interesting smells for curious puppies to explore.

They continued up the hill and down the other side. When they arrived at the dam on the other side of the hill the children took off their boots and together the puppies and children squelched around in the muddy shallow water near the edge. They weren't allowed to swim when there was no adult, even though they were all good swimmers. But they could play at the edge of the dam.

After squelching in the mud, three muddy puppies and six muddy human feet padded along the little jetty that stretched out to the middle of the dam. They sat on the edge and dangled their feet in the water. The water was cool even though the summer sun was quite warm.

After a while the puppies started to fidget and they pulled at their leashes to keep going. The children dried off their feet with their socks and slipped their boots back on. In summer they wore boots because of the snakes. They knew that all the snakes in Tasmania were poisonous and it was the summer time that the snakes were out and about.

Before they left the dam the puppies had a drink at the edge of the dam. Then they climbed over the hill once again. When they got to the top they saw that a motorbike with a big yellow pouch on either side had pulled up at the gate of their farm.

"The mail's here!" yelled Olingah. "Race you to the mailbox. Last one there's a rotten egg." Olingah took off down the hill. Flea ran excitedly beside him, ears flapping and tongue dripping. Olingah's older sisters followed quickly after him. Even though Leezah who was ten and Skye who was eight were both faster than their six-year-old brother, the older sisters let Olingah win. When they got to the green mailbox they saw that there was a bundle of mail sticking out of it.

There was the usual assortment of bills and bank statements, papers, and magazines for Dr and Mr Fitzgerald. There was a letter in a blue envelope addressed to Rommy and Flip. And there at the bottom of the pile was a yellow envelope that made the children's eyes open wide with excitement. It was addressed to:

Olingah, Leezah and Skye-Maree
Fitzgerald
Fellowship Farm
Kellyton
Tasmania

A visit is planned

The children hurried through the little gate at the front of the house and went around the back. They unhooked the leashes from the puppies' collars and hung the leashes on the hooks in the boot room. They dumped the rest of the mail on the kitchen table. Then they sat down on the back verandah to open the unexpected yellow letter.

Inside there was a piece of paper covered in stickers and writing in purple pen. The letter said:

Dear Cousins,

How are you? We are very well. We only have one week left of school. Then we are coming to Fellowship Farm. Can you believe we will be together for two whole weeks?? We can't wait to see your new puppies.

Lots of love,
Nick and Annissa

"Nick and Annissa are coming to Fellowship Farm!?" exclaimed Leezah. She ran inside to the kitchen and picked up the radio. She pressed down on the button and said: "Base to Mobile One. Over." She waited for a minute but there was no answer. Her father must be away from the Ute. She tried again. This time Leezah said: "Base to Mobile Two. Over." Her mum's voice came back "Mobile Two to base. Over."

"Mum, are Nick and Annissa coming to stay??? Over."

"Yes they are. We'll talk more at lunch time honey. Over."

The Fitzgerald children were ecstatic.

As Olingah and Skye danced and yelled in the background Leezah tried to keep her voice steady as she pressed the radio button one last time to say: "Over and out".

At about 12 o'clock their mum came back to the farmhouse from the back paddocks. She parked her orange Ute out the front of the farmhouse and was immediately swamped by three very happy children. Dr Fitzgerald pretended to be frightened. She quickly locked her door, rolled up the window and covered her head with her arms. The children laughed and banged on the window. Their mum quickly slid over to the passenger door and jumped out of the Ute. She ran around the Ute and leaped the low dilapidated fence. Then she ran to the back of the house with three giggling children chasing her.

As she pulled her boots off Leezah, Skye and Olingah caught up with her and wrapped their arms around her. Immediately there were a hundred questions fired at Dr Fitzgerald. "Is it true?" "When are they coming?" "Can we meet them at the airport?" "How long are they staying?" "Are Aunty Jen and Uncle Karim coming with them?"

"How about this," suggested their mum. "Leezah, you make a salad. Skye you get the things out of the fridge for me to make the sandwiches. Olingah you set the table. I'll go have a shower and get ready to go to the surgery. And then we'll all have some lunch and I will answer ALL your questions!" The children hurried to the kitchen and left Dr Fitzgerald to take off her boots in peace.

• • • • • • • • • • • • • • • • • • • •

The lunch was all ready when Mr Fitzgerald came in and washed his hands. So they sat down together to eat. The children were DYING to get answers to their questions but they knew that if they rushed their mum she would just make them wait even longer. When everyone had taken a sandwich and some salad from the dishes in the middle of the table and started to eat, Dr Fitzgerald began to explain.

The children's Aunty Jen and Uncle Karim were going away for two weeks. So they had organized with the Fitzgeralds for their children – Nick who was eleven and Annissa who was six – to come and stay at the farm for that time. Dr and Mr Fitzgerald had decided to keep it as a surprise. So until the letter arrived the children had no idea that their cousins were coming to stay.

"When do they arrive?" asked Skye

"Next Monday at 8:00am," said Mummy. "They are coming by themselves. We will go in to Launceston to meet them at the airport and bring them straight back to the farm. At the end their stay Aunty Jen and Uncle Karim will come for a weekend and then take them back to Sydney."

"Fantastic!"

After lunch Dr Fitzgerald left for the town where she worked each afternoon as a vet. Mr Fitzgerald went up to the shed where he spent the afternoon working on the tractor engine. The children played, and planned for their cousins visit, until at 4:30 their dad came to get them for the feeding out.

Off to the airport

For the rest of the week the children took it in turns to color in the day on the calendar. On Monday the whole family woke up an hour earlier than usual – at five o'clock. They gathered in the living room for morning prayers. Daddy said a special prayer for journeys because four of his favorite people were going to be on the road to Launceston and back.

After prayers was breakfast, then morning chores. When all the animals were fed the children changed out of their farm clothes. A trip to Launceston was a special occasion and greeting their cousins at the airport was a very special occasion so they all put on their best clothes.

Leezah, Skye-Maree and Olingah each had one outfit that they wore on special days, like Nineteen Day Feasts, Holy Days or parties. They called their good clothes their "Feast clothes". Leezah's feast dress was a present from her great grandma. It was dark green with tiny yellow puppies scampering across the bottom and on the pockets. It reached all the way down to her ankles. She put it on and pulled her long black hair into two pigtails.

Skye's feast dress had little circles on the straps and waist, called sequins, that sparkled in the light. Her dress was pink. It reached down to her knees with a little bit of a petticoat underneath. She had picked it out when her Aunty Alex took her to Hobart earlier in the year. Aunty Alex loved all her nieces and nephews but she had a special friendship with Skye. Aunty Alex had been with Skye's mummy while Skye was being born and had chosen her name. So sometimes she did special things with Skye. Aunty Alex loved frills and bows and things that sparkled. Skye also had some clips that matched her dress. She clipped them into her dark frizzy hair.

Olingah's feast clothes were also very smart. He had some navy blue pants with a little leather belt – just like his Daddy's. And he had a pink t-shirt with long sleeves. Around the neck were little roses. Whenever he wore it Daddy called Olingah the rose among the roses. Olingah's feast clothes came from the Kellyton market that was held every Sunday. The

Fitzgerald family went each week to the market. Sometimes, for a special treat, they hitched the big old Clydesdale horse to the cart, and rode in with horse and cart.

When they were all dressed they went out to the living room. Mummy helped Olingah brush the knots out of his shoulder length fine brown hair while his sisters swirled around making their feast dresses swish out. The girls imagined they were ballet dancers.

"Okay, let's get our things into the car kids," said Mummy playfully patting Olingah's bottom with the brush before putting it away.

The drive into Launceston took a long time so they each took a pillow and one toy. Mummy had packed a bag with some water, crackers and fruit. Olingah carried it out to the orange Ute. They gave their dad a big hug and a kiss and piled into the car. For the journey to Launceston they could all sit by a window – Skye in the front seat and Leezah and Olingah in the back. On the way back someone would need to sit in the middle of the front seat and in the middle of the back seat. But the excitement of having the cousins in the car would stop them feeling carsick.

"Who has their seatbelt on?" asked Mum, before starting the car.

"Me," said three Fitzgerald voices.

"Good. Let's go," she said, and turned the key.

The orange Ute pulled out of the farm property onto the dirt road. Daddy shut the blue gate behind them and waved as they drove away. They opened their windows and felt the cool morning breeze on their faces as they drove past the other farms. Soon they reached Kellyton township. They passed the Animal Hospital where Dr Fitzgerald would go to work later that afternoon. They continued past the bakery and the newsagent that was already open. The rest of the shops in the town were still closed.

Then the Fitzgerald family took the road that led to Launceston. As they drove they played eye-spy, then car-cricket. They sang some songs and then they just sat quietly watching the familiar scenery go by. After more than one hour of driving Skye saw a sign with an airplane on it. Next to the airplane was the number 3.

"Nearly there!" she said.

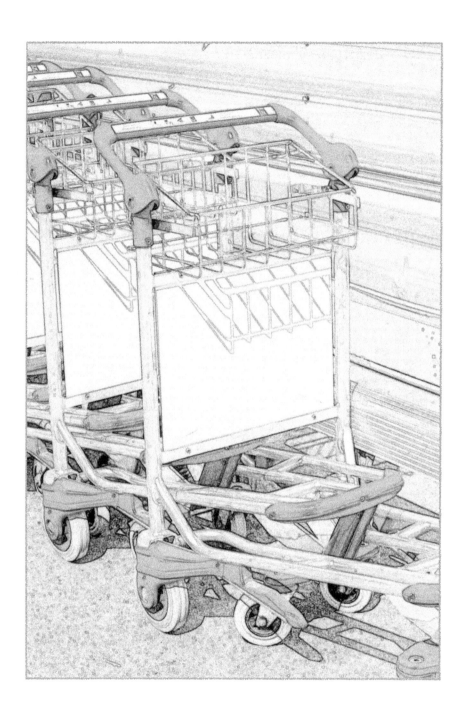

Half a dozen cousins

Dr Fitzgerald turned off the main road and into the airport. The children could not sit still. They pulled at their seatbelts so they could sit higher in their seats. They strained their necks toward the terminal as their mum drove past. Dr Fitzgerald pulled up at the gate of the car park. She pressed a button on a grey box and a ticket came out. She pulled the ticket out of the slot and the gate swung up. The car drove through.

The car park was about half full. They found a spot to park. As soon as the car stopped, the children threw off their seat belts and jumped out of the car. The chattered excitedly as their mum locked the doors. Then they hurried out of the car park, across the pedestrian crossing and towards the terminal.

One wall was made completely of glass. In the middle were doors that slid open when the children came close. When the children were smaller they thought the electronic sliding doors were magic. The children skipped into the terminal with Dr Fitzgerald following behind.

They looked up at the television set that had information about flight arrival and departure.

"Which flight are they on?" asked Leezah

"Q 654 from Sydney, due for arrival at 8:00a.m. " replied Mummy.

Leezah looked for information about that flight. It was hard to see because the television was high up. Suddenly she saw Q 654. "It's landed! It's landed!" she yelled grabbing her sister in excitement and nearly ripping some sequins off Skye's feast dress.

The four Fitzgeralds hurried through the doors that led toward the runway. The children leaped down the cement stairs two at a time. Just at the end Olingah mistimed his jump and landed hard on his hands and knees. His sisters were at his side instantly.

Olingah struggled with the tears that were nearly bursting out of his eyes. This was not a time to be crying, but his hands were grazed and bleeding, and they hurt. He got slowly to his feet and discovered two big holes in his Feast pants. The holes revealed bleeding knees.

Olingah looked up at his mum and the tears brimmed over and spilled down his little brown face. Mummy put her arm around Olingah and they all went more slowly down the last flight of stairs to the gate.

There were other people waiting anxiously for their friends and relatives and they all watched happily as the door of the plane swung open. The stairs on wheels were driven up to the plane door and the passengers began to appear and make their way down the stairs.

Olingah's scrapes were forgotten as the three of them pressed their noses against the glass of the windows concentrating all their attention on spotting their cousins. A long stream of people came out of the plane, across the tarmac and through the gate. Friends and relatives hugged and cried and laughed and moved up from the gate to go and collect luggage. But still no cousins for the Fitzgerald children.

"Where ARE they?" begged Skye of no one in particular.

Finally the stream of passengers stopped coming. No more passengers were leaving the plane. And yet the cousins had not appeared. Leezah and Skye and Olingah's hearts felt heavy with disappointment. They turned to their mum.

"Where are they?" Skye asked again looking at her mum.

Mummy stood quietly for a long time, pretending to look very worried. "Um, maybe they fell out during the flight?" she suggested. Olingah's eyes opened wide with fear at the thought. "Or maybe they fell asleep inside the plane and don't know they've arrived."

"So what will happen?" asked Leezah.

"Well, they might just get flown back to Sydney with the next lot of passengers," said Mummy trying hard to look serious.

Just then the children heard someone calling their names. They turned around to face the tarmac again. Two children who were being accompanied by a hostess were waving madly as they walked from the plane toward the gate.

As soon as they stepped inside the gate Annissa and Nick were swamped in cousin arms.

"What took you so long?" asked Skye as she squeezed her little cousin Annissa.

"Because we were traveling by ourselves we had to wait 'til last so the hostess could bring us over the tarmac," replied Nick.

"We thought you fell out of the plane," said Leezah. The cousins started to giggle at the thought as they climbed the stairs to the luggage collection area.

An unhappy surprise

Dr Fitzgerald's name was Rosemary. Leezah, Skye and Olingah's grandmother, who was Dr Fitzgerald's mother, called her Rosie. But everyone else called her Rommy. To Nick and Annissa she was Aunt Rommy. Mr Fitzgerald's real name was George but no-one ever called him that. He was known to everyone as Flip. So Nick and Annissa called him Uncle Flip.

"You all wait here for the baggage," suggested Dr Fitzgerald. "I'll go and get the car."

"Okay Aunt Rommy," said Nick.

"Can I come with you and do the ticket?" asked Olingah

"Of course honey."

Olingah and his mum went across the road, and through the car park to the little office in the middle of the car park. Dr Fitzgerald pulled the parking ticket out of her bag and gave it to the man inside. Then she handed him five dollars. He slid the ticket through a machine and passed it back to her.

"Thank you Ma'am," he said.

"Thank you," said Dr Fitzgerald.

They found the car and drove to the exit gate. Olingah climbed onto his mum's lap and leaned out the window. He stuck the ticket in the slot. The machine swallowed the card and the gate swung up. They drove through.

They pulled up in front of the terminal. The baggage had already arrived and the cousins were waiting by the curb chattering and laughing. Dr Fitzgerald put her niece and nephew's bags into the back of the Ute and the children climbed in. Dr Fitzgerald glanced at the sky. There were dark clouds gathering. She decided to cover the back of the Ute with the tarpaulin. She quickly hooked it on all sides and got back into the car.

"So, who's ready to go to Fellowship Farm?" she asked turning to the five happy faces in the car.

"ME!" they all yelled, as the Ute pulled away from the curb and drove out of the airport.

As Dr Fitzgerald drove quickly along the highway the children caught up on each other's news. They had not seen each other since May, which was seven months ago. All the cousins had gathered in Hobart when their great grandmother had turned ninety. The Fitzgeralds had gone from Kellyton with their mum. Annissa and Nick had gone from Sydney with Aunty Jen- Dr Fitzgerald's sister. And the five cousins living in Papua New Guinea came with Dr Fitzgerald's brother, Gray and his wife Labu. It was a wonderful week together. But they had not seen each other since, so there was a lot to talk about.

As the children chatted Dr Fitzgerald focused on the driving. She noticed that there were a lot of log trucks on the road which made her nervous. As the road became two lanes in either direction one of the big trucks came roaring up behind them. As it drove past, a rock on the road got lifted by its wheel. The rock came flying toward the front window. Instantly the windscreen shattered.

Dr Fitgerald got a huge shock and swung the wheel of the car to the left, away from the truck. The car veered off the road and spun on the gravel. Leezah and Nick screamed.

A flat tyre and an unplanned picnic

The car skidded to a stop right before a telegraph pole. Dr Fitzgerald turned quickly to check the startled children. No-one had been hurt. She offered a silent prayer of thanks. Annissa and Olingah started to cry quietly. Dr Fitzgerald took some deep breaths. A hissing sound was coming from outside the car. She took off her seatbelt and stepped out of the car. She walked around it checking for damage. The front left tyre was getting rapidly flatter. It was punctured.

Dr Fitzgerald was shaking now as she started to realize how close they had come to being in a serious accident. She got back into the car. She looked at each of the frightened little faces and asked: "How are you feeling?" No-one replied. "Let's sing some prayers, and then we'll work out what to do next," she suggested.

"Is there any remover of difficulties, save God. Say! Praised be God. He is God. All are

His servants and all abide by His bidding." They sang the prayer nine times.

Then Dr Fitzgerald turned to face the children again. "Now, a rock from that truck smashed our windscreen and we have a flat tyre," she said with a gentle smile. "It won't take long to change the tyre. And we'll push out some of the glass so I can see. Then we'll get back to the farm and everything will be fine, okay?"

"Okay Aunt Rommy," said Nick.

"You'll all need to climb out while I jack up the car," she said and the children obeyed.

Dr Fitzgerald found her tool box, placed the jack under the car and jacked it up. She took off the flat tyre. The children stood by the car watching. Dr Fitzgerald suggested they get the food from out of the car and have a little picnic while they waited. Skye and Leezah took the rug covering the back seat of the car and set it out on the grass by the road side. They put the crackers and fruit and water and everyone sat down for an unplanned picnic. The children started to feel better and as they did, an attack of giggles hit them.

Once they had started they didn't want to stop so they started to tell each other jokes they had heard at school.

"How do you get an elephant into the fridge?" asked Skye "Open the door and push," she answered her own joke. Everybody groaned and giggled.

"How do you get a tiger into the fridge?" she asked.

"Open the door and push?" answered Nick

"NO! Open the door, take the elephant out, then push," said Skye.

Leezah rolled her eyes. "Your jokes are weird Skye!" Then Leezah started to tell a joke. "There were three friends, Alice, Sarah and Jack..." and the jokes went on.

Soon Dr Fitzgerald brushed the gravel from her hands and knees and put away the tools. She grabbed an old ice-cream container from under her seat and started to tap out some of the shattered glass over the driver's seat. As she did this some lightening shot across the sky. A few seconds later some thunder followed.

"Alrighty, into the car everyone," she said, when she had made a decent sized hole in the shattered glass. Dr Fitzgerald pulled slowly onto the road and began to drive. The children were feeling much more relaxed now and were beginning to enjoy the adventure.

It was then that it started to pour with rain.

Wet but well

Two and a half hours later the five cold, tired and damp cousins arrived at Fellowship Farm with one very very wet, cold and tired mummy/aunty. It was not raining at the farm. Dr Fitzgerald stopped at the farmhouse to let the children out and to take the bags inside. Then she drove the car up to the shed. As she parked the Ute she radioed to Mr Fitzgerald. He came in from the farm to greet them and hear of their adventures.

As the children and Dr Fitzgerald showered and changed, Mr Fitzgerald made some hot drinks. "So welcome to the Tasmanian summer," he grinned at Nick and Annissa as the children came into the living room where Mr Fitzgerald was putting the tray of drinks on the table. They gave their uncle a big hug and he lifted them both off the ground. When he put them down again he staggered around clutching his back. "Ow ow," he moaned, pretending to be hurt. "You're way too big to be helicopter hugged. When did you two get so big??" he asked, still holding his back and moaning.

"Yes, I'm already THIS big," said Annissa putting her hand on top of her head.

Uncle Flip opened his eyes wide with astonishment. As they all sat down to have their drinks, Mr Fitzgerald said with a serious face: "So your mother, your aunty, tells me that you saw a UFO with aliens in it on the way home?"

Leezah, Skye and Olingah knew that their Daddy was teasing and they played along with him.

"Yes," said Leezah, "there were three hundred of them and they took us for a ride to space."

"You went for a ride in space ship and you didn't get me???" said Daddy pretending to be hurt.

"Yup," laughed Skye, "but they said you can go next time...if you're good." Daddy promised he would try to be good.

It was getting close to the time that needed to go to the surgery. She hugged each of the children and walked up to the shed to get the motorbike and fill it with petrol. Mr Fitzgerald headed back out to the farm. And the children took Annissa and Nick to meet Flea, Flex, and Fizz.

After everyone had been snuggled and licked by Flea, Flex and Fizz, the children attached the leashes and they all headed up to the apple orchard. The apple orchard was full of old apple trees. No-one paid it much attention these days but delicious apples still grew there in the autumn and it was also a perfect place for hide and seek.

The apple orchard was popular for other reasons too. In one of the big old trees there were some strong ropes firmly tied. The children climbed up the tree and took it in turns to grab hold of the rope and jump. They swished through the air back and forth back and forth until the rope was nearly still. Then they jumped off and threw it back up to the next person.

As they climbed up the tree and got ready to jump the puppies became very excited. They stood under the branch and yipped and barked and ran in circles. The children were scared the puppies would get hit by the end of the rope as it swung, so Olingah climbed back down the tree and held onto the puppies while Nick jumped first.

Then Nick held the puppies while Skye jumped. After each person had a turn to swing, they held the puppies for the next. When everyone had had what seemed like hundreds of swings, the children decided to play hide and seek. Skye and Annissa counted first while the others hid.

They scattered through the orchard. Leezah lay down in the long grass and was completely hidden. Nick hid behind one of the bigger trees on the very edge of the orchard near the fence. Olingah quickly climbed one of the trees and hid in the branches.

"One, two, three, four, five, six,..." counted Skye and Annissa slowly, all the way to forty. Then, holding hands they went looking for the others. They spotted Olingah first. "One three two, we see you," sang Skye

"One two three, you got me," sang Olingah back, clambering down the tree. The next person to be found was Nick. He was trying to be tricky and run from his hiding spot to another tree. But he was spotted by the quick eyes of his sister.

Neither Nick nor Olingah had seen where Leezah had hidden. So all four of them hunted for her. They looked all over the orchard, but nobody found her in the long grass right near where the girls had counted. Finally Skye had an idea. She knelt down to the puppies and unleashed them. "Where's Leezah? Where's Leezah?" she asked in an excited voice. The puppies dashed around in mad circles, happy to be off their leashes. "Where's Leezah?" all the children asked. Just then they heard a short high whistle. The puppies dashed off in the direction it had come from.

Soon the children heard the laughter of Leezah being licked to death and saw the grass moving where she was tumbling over and over with three excited puppies clambering all over her.

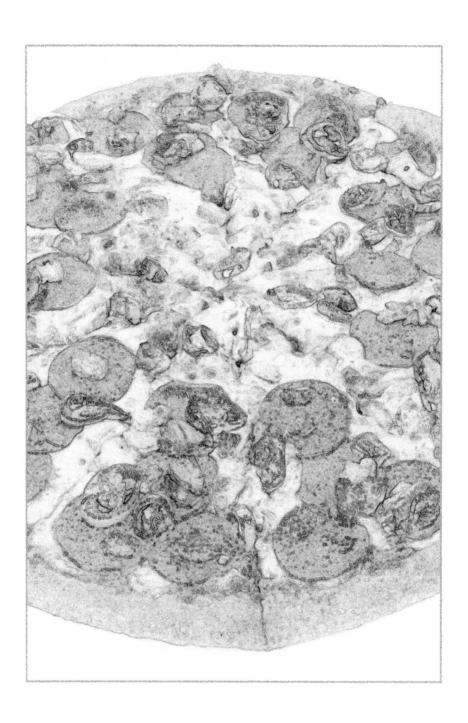

Cold sandwiches and hot pizza

"Good hiding spot Sister!" said Olingah as Leezah stood up and brushed grass and twigs from her clothes.

The children had been playing in the orchard for a long time and it was already late afternoon. "I'm starving," said Olingah and everyone agreed that they were very hungry. They put the leashes back on the puppies and left the orchard. As they walked through the paddocks toward the farmhouse they heard the sound of the Ute coming closer.

Then it appeared at the top of the hill and Mr Fitzgerald stuck his head out of the window. "I thought I might find my lovelies here," he smiled. "Been playing in the orchard?"

The children nodded. "Come on jump on. Your sandwiches and fruit have been ready for ages. They'll be getting cold," he added.

"Sandwiches and fruit are meant to be cold Dad!" laughed Skye as the children climbed onto the back of the Ute.

"Oh," said Daddy, "well that's lucky."

The children held on tight as Mr Fitzgerald drove down the hill. The wind blew in their hair and faces. They felt like they were flying.

When they arrived at the farmhouse Mr Fitzgerald said: "Now you go have those cold sandwiches and I'll be back in half an hour to collect my helpers for feeding out okay?"

The children waved goodbye and went through the little farmhouse gate, around the house and up the back steps to the verandah. They took off their boots and washed their hands. Their lunch was waiting on the table, covered in a lacy white cloth to keep away the flies.

"Yum! Chocolate milk!" said Leezah, noticing that instead of fruit juice there were five cups of her favorite drink.

While the children ate and drank they talked about their favorite foods.

"Would you rather have a whole room full of watermelon or a whole room full of pineapple?" asked Annissa.

"Pineapple"

"No way, definitely watermelon."

"Me too, I'd want watermelon."

"Okay, " said Skye, " would you rather have a magic tree that gave you as many smarties as you wanted, or a magic tree that gave you as many chocolate freckles as you want?"

"I want smarties."

"I want freckles and smarties."

"I'd rather have a magic tree that grew musk sticks," added Leezah. Musk sticks were her favorite.

After lunch Nick and Leezah quickly washed the dishes. As soon as they had finished there was a horn honk from out the front of the house. The children scrambled to put their boots on and ran to the Ute. They climbed on the back and headed for the haybarn.

Mr Fitzgerald backed the Ute hard against the stack of hay. The three Fitzgerald children climbed the slippery haystack, pushing and pulling each other up. Annissa and Nick followed their example and soon they were all on the top pushing the bales down to Mr Fitzgerald who was standing on the Ute ready to stack them.

The feeding out was very quick with five ready helpers on the back of the Ute, and soon the cows were all fed and happily munching away. Mr Fitzgerald drove back to the shed and the children attended to the evening chores. As they arrived back at the farmhouse Dr Fitzgerald greeted them with a big floury smile. She was making pizza dough.

"Hoorah!!" shouted the children, "Pizza!!"

"Can we help?"

"Of couse. Are your hands clean?"

"Yes," they all replied. They had washed at the outside toilet before coming in.

Together they chopped vegetables and sliced salami, grated cheese, opened bottles of pizza sauce and cans of pineapple. Then they spread the pizza dough with all that they had prepared and put them in the oven to cook.

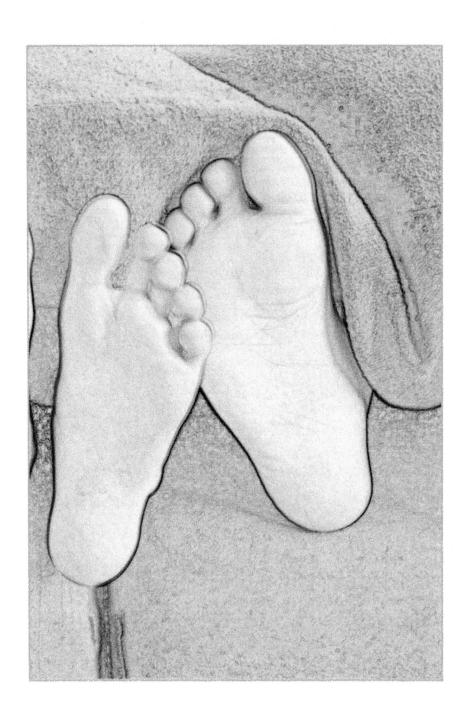

A tent for five

Dr. Fitzgerald had made the beds up in the spare room and taken Nick and Annissa's bags in there. While the pizzas cooked all the children showered and put on their pajamas. Then Nick and Annissa came into their cousins' room and they set up the Chinese Checkers board for a game.

While they played Leezah had an idea. "Let's ask Mummy and Daddy if we can make a tent in here and all sleep together tonight?"

"Yeah!" said Skye, "Let's finish this game and then go ask. Come on Annissa, your turn."

But before the Chinese Checkers was over the pizza was cooked and Daddy appeared in doorway of the bedroom to call them for dinner. Three big pizzas were in the middle of the dining table and seven hungry people gathered around to devour them. While they ate, Nick said, "Aunty Rommy, can you speak Italian?"

Aunty Rommy's mouth was full of mushrooms, cheese, capsicum and salami. She shook her head.

"Uncle Flip?"

"No, Nick, can you?"

"Yes," boasted Nick. He pulled a long string of melted cheese from his plate to above his head and said, "Mozzarella! Mozzarella!! Mozzarella!!"

While they ate Leezah asked if they could make a tent and sleep in it together. Mummy looked at Daddy, who looked at Mummy and shrugged his shoulders. "Why not?" said Dad. "There's no school tomorrow."

"There's no school for five whole weeks!" said Skye-Maree.

"Good, well you'll have time to catch up on the sleep you're not going to get tonight then," replied Dad, getting up from the table and gathering the empty plates.

When everyone had finished Mummy said that she and Daddy would wash up tonight. "Thanks Mum. Thanks Dad. Thanks Aunt Rommy. Thanks Uncle Flip," said the children and ran off to brush their teeth. When teeth were brushed and flossed, Leezah and Nick pulled the biggest sheets they could find out of the linen cupboard and the children set to work to turn the bedroom into a huge tent.

They tied one end of the sheet to the bunk and the other to the cupboard. Then they clipped and tied and hitched and fixed until the tent had four walls. Mattresses went in next followed by quilts and pillows. The tent was complete. Except for one thing. Leezah went out to the kitchen where her Dad was folding laundry on the kitchen table.

"Is it okay if we use this in our tent?" she asked, pointing to the torch attached to the fridge by a magnet.

Daddy nodded. Leezah took the torch and went back to the bedroom. The others were all inside the tent. Leezah turned off the bedroom light and everyone cried out. Then she turned on the torch and shone it through the door of the tent. "Don't worry dears. I'll keep you safe," said Leezah in a funny high pitched voice, "... from the Dark Monsters," she added in a deep growling voice and flashed the torch back and forth. The children giggled and screamed and beat Leezah with pillows. Soon a full scale pillow war was taking place.

The pillow war was interrupted a few minutes later by the call to prayer. The children came panting out of their tent. They sat themselves on the couch, chairs and floor of the living room and settled down. Annissa and Nick crossed their arms and closed their eyes. Nick and Annissa chanted beautiful prayers in Persian that their father had taught them. Each of the children sang and read prayers and Writings.

When they had finished Dr Fitzgerald thanked the children for their beautiful reverence. She told them they could add a sticker each next to reverence and a sticker each next to unity on the virtues chart. When the children had stuck their stickers they came and said goodnight. It was still early but they wanted to go to bed early for some reason!

Soon giggles and squeals and pillow fights could be heard coming from the bedroom.

Off to market...

The first week together flew past filled with fun and laughter, and lack of sleep. Before they knew it, it was Sunday. On Sunday the Fitzgerald family always went to the market. It was a good opportunity to get fresh fruit and vegetables as well as other things. There was usually a local group called *Michelangela* playing live music, and it was also time to chat with other people in their town and catch up on news. Most often they drove to the market in the orange Ute. But sometimes, they went another way.

In the paddock behind the big shed that housed the tractors and Utes, there were three horses. The two smaller horses were for riding. The third horse was very very big and hairy. Her name was Bonnie. She was a Clydesdale and very strong. Mr Fitzgerald and the children went through the gate to the horse paddock and closed it behind them. They clicked their tongues and whistled. The three horses came trotting up the paddock. They knew what was waiting for them.

When the horses came close the children held out their hands. They tucked their thumbs underneath so they wouldn't get munched. On each little palm sat an apple. The horses snuffled the children's hands and then crunched the apples with their strong teeth. While they ate Mr Fitzgerald put a halter over Bonnie's head and attached a rope to it like a dog's lead. The horses liked the apples and they came sniffing and snorting at the children looking for more. Nick and Annissa were a little afraid and they stepped back toward the gate.

"The horses won't hurt you," said Olingah to his cousins. "They just want more apples."

Leezah, Skye and Olingah gave the horses a rub saying, "That's all greedies, off you go now." Mr Fitzgerald led Bonnie through the gate and Leezah shut it behind him. The other horses hung their heads over the gate nibbling at the longer grass on the other side and snorting air through their big round nostrils.

"Who wants a ride on Bonnie?" asked Dad.

"Me!" said Olingah. Daddy hoisted him up. Skye was next. Annissa and Nick wanted to as well but they were a bit cautious. "Maybe next time," they said.

"It's okay," said Leezah. "Once you get used to Bonnie you'll feel as safe with her as you do with Fizz. Just take some time to get to know her." Leezah walked along with her cousins.

They took the horse to the big shed. Annissa and Nick helped their cousins wipe the cart down. It was a few weeks since they had used it and it was covered in dust. Some spiders had made their home in it too. Then Mr Fitzgerald put Bonnie's harness on and attached her to the cart. The children climbed onto the cart. Skye and Mr Fitzgerald sat up the front with Skye holding the reins. She clicked her tongue. "Gittup Bon," she said and the horse moved slowly forward. The cart bumped along behind with four happy children in the back.

Bonnie pulled the cart slowly down the hill from the shed to the farmhouse. Dr Fitzgerald handed out hats and put a big empty basket and three empty cotton bags in the back of the cart. Mr Fitzgerald stretched his hand down and said "M'lady". Dr Fitzgerald bobbed her head: "M'lord", took his hand and pulled herself up to the seat at the front of the cart.

She took her wallet from out of her back jeans pocket and threw it into the basket in the back.

"Okay Miss Skye-Maree Martha Amelia Fitzgerald. To Market!"

"Gittup," said Skye again to Bonnie and the old Clydesdale pulled away from the farmhouse fence, plodded through the farm gate and out onto the road.

Once they were on the open road Skye flicked the reins and Bonnie picked up the pace to a slow trot. The children in the back held on to the side of the cart and enjoyed the ride.

Annissa and Nick felt their hearts bursting with happiness. They loved their cousins. They loved Fellowship Farm and their Aunt Rommy and Uncle Flip. They thought happily of the days that stretched ahead of them and wished they would never end.

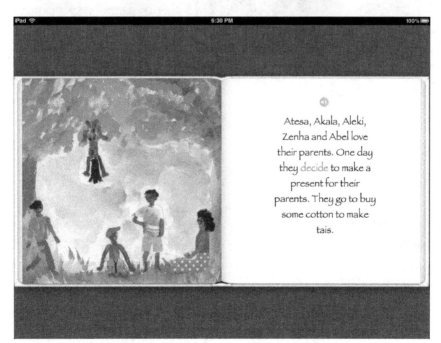

Fellowship Farm

Volume 1: Books 1 - 3

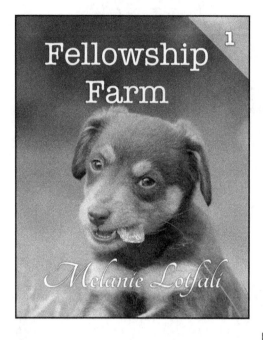

Leezah, Skye-Maree and Olingah Fitzgerald live with their parents on Fellowship Farm. In the first book of the Fellowship Farm series, you will meet the children and learn about their daily activities on the farm. There is a lot to be done each day: pillow fights, morning prayers, pig feeding and school bus riding. They help their dad feed the cows, add stickers to their virtues poster and learn to deal with bullies.

Then you will join the Fitzgerald children on their many adventures with puppies, snake bites, treasure hunts, bonfires, camping by the sea, and tree houses. And as they go they sometimes practice their virtues, and sometimes forget...

Suitable for independent readers aged 8-12 years; parent-read from six years. Order online from print-on-demand services, and digitally from the iBookstore or Kindle.

Fellowship Farm

Volume 2: Books 4 - 6

Leezah, Skye-Maree and Olingah Fitzgerald live with their parents on Fellowship Farm. In the first volume of the Fellowship Farm series, you met the children and learned about their daily activities on the farm.

In this the second volume the Fitzgerald children are visited by their cousins, Nick and

Anisa. Together they travel by horse and cart to the market, attend the 19 Day Feast, go camping, find a pirate map and treasure, as well as experience the intensity of crisis and victory when Olingah's life is put in serious danger.

Suitable for independent readers aged 8-12 years; parent-read from six years. Order online from print-on-demand services, and digitally from the iBookstore or Kindle.

Fellowship Farm

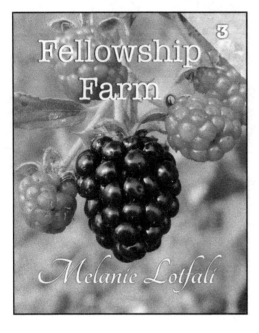

Volume 3: Books 7 - 9

In this, the third volume of stories about Leezah, Skye-Maree and Olingah Fitzgerald who live with their parents on Fellowship Farm, the children set out with joy to go blackberry picking.

But an unexpected turn of events at the river makes them fear for the lives of their puppies. Ayyám-i-Há follows with serving, teaching, gifts, treasure hunts as well as the challenge of bullying for Skye-Maree. After Ayyám-i-Há comes an opportunity to visit their eccentric Uncle Jack who takes them to the chocolate factory, aquatic centre and gives them many other treats both spiritual and edible!

Suitable for independent readers aged 8-12 years; parent-read from six years. Order online from print-on-demand services, and digitally from the iBookstore or Kindle.

Fellowship Farm

Volume 4: Books 10 - 12

In the fourth volume of stories about Leezah, Skye-Maree and Olingah Fitzgerald of Fellowship Farm they prepare for the annual Naw Ruz Mahta River Boat Race. There are some unexpected hitches.

Skye-Maree and Olingah learn about loyalty and sacrifice as they work out how to respond to the challenges they face. Soon after Naw Ruz winter sets in and the family rug up and head for the ski slopes. Along the way they experience the life-threatening danger of losing unity, the challenge of learning to ski, the power of prayer, and patience in the face of frustration. They meet funny Magic, the back to front panda, and suffer some bruises. Their patience is well rewarded when their parents announce that a dear wish of the children is to be fulfilled.

Suitable for independent readers aged 8-12 years; parent-read from six years. Order online from print-on-demand services, and digitally from the iBookstore or Kindle.

Unity in Diversity

This brightly illustrated picture book contains five simple stories for young readers. They foster an understanding of the oneness of the human race and celebrate its diversity within that unity.

Likening the human race to various colored cotton in a woven cloth, various fruits on the tree of life, stars in the heavens, members of one body, and different notes in one perfect chord, the stories use the concrete to teach the abstract.

Young readers will enjoy the bright colors and simple text as they develop their understanding of the unity and diversity of the human race.

Ideal for children aged 4-8 years.
Order online from print-on-demand services, and digitally from the iBookstore. Translated into French, Portuguese, Romanian, Tetum, and Mongolian.

The Big Story

The Big Story explains the way in which the divinely ordained and guided process that has brought human beings into existence has taken place gradually over time and space. It shows that the concepts of evolution and creation are not mutually exclusive.

Science and religion are shown to be two windows on one reality, two knowledge systems that when properly understood, function as one cohesive whole.

This book is most suitable for readers 14 years and older. Younger readers will enjoy the bright and informative illustrations but will require support to understand the text.

Suitable for independent readers aged 14+ years; with assistance from 12+. Order online from print-on-demand services, and digitally from the iBookstore.

Dr Melanie Lotfali

Author of The Fitzgeralds of Fellowship Farm series and Unity in Diversity series.

Melanie Lotfali PhD is a graduate of the Australian College of Journalism in Professional Writing for Children. She is the author of eighteen books of fiction and non-fiction for children and the illustrator of five.

Melanie has taught spiritual education classes for children for the past twenty years in five countries and is currently an active animator and trainer of animators for the Junior Youth Spiritual Empowerment Program. She is a qualified counselor and classroom teacher, and for over six years facilitated violence prevention and respectful relationships programs in high schools.

Much of her childhood was spent on the farms, beaches and mountains of Tasmania, where the Fellowship Farm series is set. As an adult she spent four years in Siberia and four years in East Timor as a pioneer.

She currently lives in Lismore, Australia, with her family.

Michael Cohen

Author of The Big Story and publisher of all Michelangela books.

Michael Cohen graduated as a Computer Systems Engineer in 1990 and worked for many years in software design and informations systems. He changed careers in 2008 to become a registered nurse working in the area of Mental Health and Alcohol & Other Drugs.

Michael has been a keen participant in and advocate of the programs offered by **The Foundation for the Application and Teaching of the Sciences** (FUNDAEC) and **Institute for Studies in Global Prosperity** (ISGP). He strives to contribute to processes and discourses leading to the progress of humankind toward a world society characterized by unity, justice and equity. A fundamental premise of Michael's worldview is that true science and true religion are necessarily in harmony, indeed are two windows on one reality. His writing seeks to promote understanding of this liberating concept and to contribute to a civilization that is ever advancing materially and spiritually.

He currently lives in Lismore, Australia, with his family.

Michelangela

website www.michelangela.com.au
email info@michelangela.com.au

To receive Michelangela's occasional product
announcements please visit our website and enter
your email address and name
via the subscribe button

CPSIA information can be obtained
at www.ICGtesting.com
Printed in the USA
LVHW101708141019
634139LV00033B/221/P